Core Connections, Course 3
Foundations for Algebra Toolkit

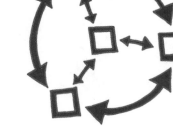

Managing Editors / Authors

Leslie Dietiker, Ph.D., Director of Curriculum (Both Editions)
Boston University
Boston, MA

Evra Baldinger (First Edition)
University of California, Berkeley
Berkeley, CA

Michael Kassarjian (Second Edition)
CPM Educational Program
Kensington, CA

Barbara Shreve (First Edition)
San Lorenzo High School
San Lorenzo, CA

Misty Nikula (Second Edition)
CPM Educational Program
Bellingham, WA

Technical Assistants: Toolkit

Hannah Coyner
Sacramento, CA

Sarah Maile
Sacramento, CA

Megan Walters
Sacramento, CA

Cover Art

Jonathan Weast
Sacramento, CA

Program Directors

Leslie Dietiker, Ph.D.
Boston University
Boston, MA

Lori Hamada
CPM Educational Program
Fresno, CA

Brian Hoey
CPM Educational Program
Sacramento, CA

Judy Kysh, Ph.D.
Departments of Education and Mathematics
San Francisco State University, CA

Tom Sallee, Ph.D.
Department of Mathematics
University of California, Davis

1 2 3 4 5 6   16 15 14 13 12 11 10

Printed in the United States of America   ISBN: 978-1-60328-096-9

Core Connections: Foundations for Algebra Course 3 Toolkit

Dear Math Student,

Welcome to your *Core Connections: Foundations for Algebra* Toolkit! It is designed to help you as you learn math throughout the school year. Inside, you will find all of the Math Notes from your textbook that have useful information about the topics you will study. You will also be able to write in your Toolkit so that you can keep track of what you have learned in your own words and refer back to those notes as you move forward.

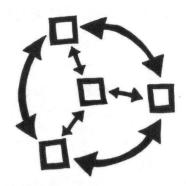

Many lessons in your math book include a prompt that asks you to think and write about the topic you are learning that day in a Learning Log. There is space in this Toolkit to write your Learning Log entries so that they are all in one place and are easy to use later. It is a good idea to leave some space between your entries so that you can add new ideas to them later, as you learn more. Note that this space has a light grid, which you can use like lined paper, as well as to help you draw diagrams or graphs.

Throughout the year, remember to make notes in your Toolkit and add examples if you find them helpful. It is important that the information on these pages—especially the Math Notes—makes sense to *you*, so be sure to highlight key information, write down important things to remember, and ask questions if something does not make sense.

Also remember that the information in your Toolkit can help you solve problems and keep track of important vocabulary words. Keep your Toolkit with you when you are working on math problems, and use it as a source of information as you move through the course.

At the end of each chapter in your textbook, there are lists of all of the Learning Log entries and Math Notes for that chapter. There are also lists of important vocabulary words. Take time as you complete each chapter to look through your Toolkit and make sure it is complete. Updating your Toolkit regularly and using it when you are studying are important student habits that will help you to be successful in this and future courses.

Have a wonderful year of learning!

The CPM Team

CHAPTER 1: PROBLEM SOLVING

Date: Lesson:	Learning Log Title:

Date: Lesson:	Learning Log Title:
	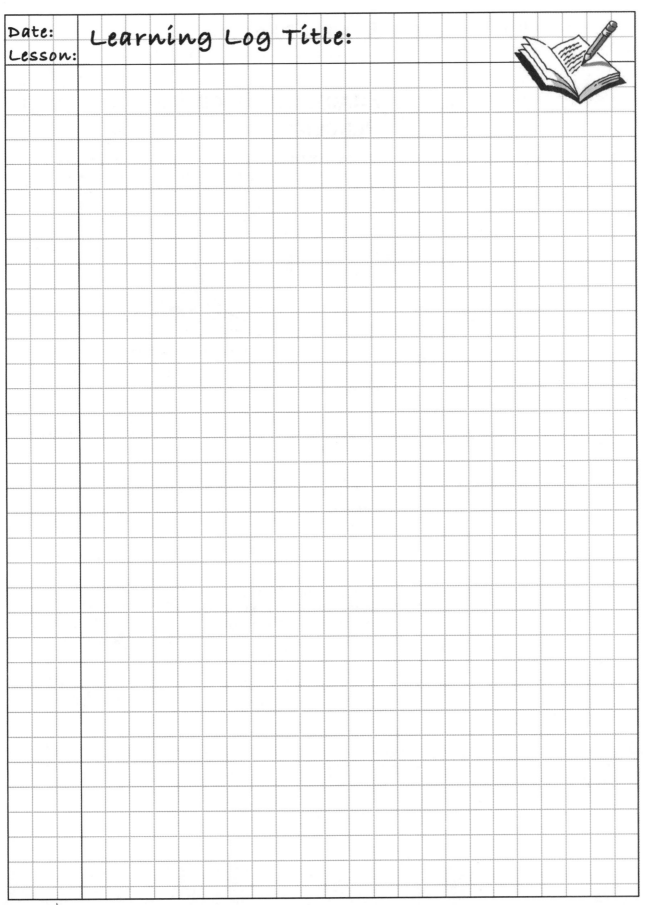

MATH NOTES

FRACTION ⇔ DECIMAL ⇔ PERCENT

The **Representations of a Portion web** diagram at right illustrates that fractions, decimals, and percents are different ways to represent a portion of a number. Portions can also be represented in words, such as "four fifths" or "twelve-fifteenths" or with diagrams.

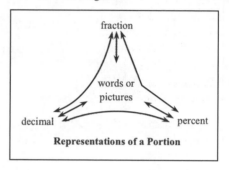

Representations of a Portion

The examples below show how to convert from one form to another.

Decimal to percent:
Multiply the decimal by 100.
$(0.34)(100) = 34\%$

Percent to decimal:
Divide the percent by 100.
$78.6\% = 78.6 \div 100 = 0.786$

Fraction to percent:
Set up an equivalent fraction using 100 as the denominator. The numerator is the percent.
$\frac{4}{5} \cdot \frac{20}{20} = \frac{80}{100} = 80\%$

Percent to fraction:
Use 100 as the denominator. Use the number in the percent as the numerator. Simplify as needed.
$22\% = \frac{22}{100} \cdot \frac{1/2}{1/2} = \frac{11}{50}$

Decimal to fraction:
Use the digits as the numerator. Use the decimal place value as the denominator. Simplify as needed.
$0.2 = \frac{2}{10} = \frac{1}{5}$

Fraction to decimal:
Divide the numerator by the denominator.
$\frac{3}{8} = 3 \div 8 = 0.375$

AXES, QUADRANTS, AND GRAPHING ON AN *XY*-COORDINATE GRAPH

Coordinate axes on a flat surface are formed by drawing vertical and horizontal number lines that meet at 0 on each number line and form a right angle (90°). The *x*- and *y*-axes help define points on a graph (called a "Cartesian Plane"). The **x-axis** is horizontal, while the **y-axis** is vertical. The *x*- and *y*-axes divide the graphing area into four sections called **quadrants**.

Numerical data can be graphed on a plane using **points**. Points on the graph are identified by two numbers in an **ordered pair** written as (x, y). The first number is the **x-coordinate** of the point, and the second number is the **y-coordinate**. The point $(0,0)$ is called the **origin**.

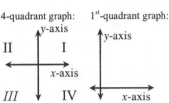

To locate the point $(3,2)$ on an *xy*-coordinate graph, go three units from the origin to the right to 3 on the horizontal axis and then, from that point, go 2 units up (using the *y*-axis scale). To locate the point $(-2,-4)$, go 2 units from the origin to the left to -2 on the horizontal axis and then 4 units down (using the *y*-axis scale).

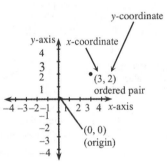

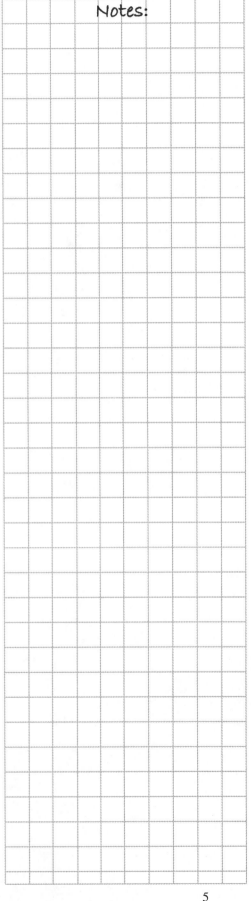

Notes:

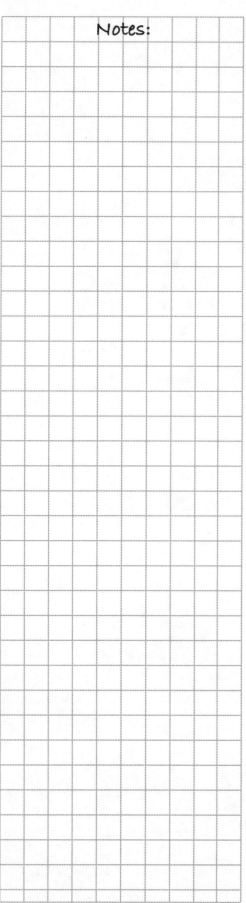

Notes:

WRITING EQUATIONS USING THE 5-D PROCESS

The 5-D Process is an organized method to help write equations and solve problems. The D's stand for Describe/Draw, Define, Do, Decide, and Declare. An example of this work is shown below.

Example Problem: The base of a rectangle is 13 centimeters longer than the height. If the perimeter is 58 centimeters, find the base and the height of the rectangle.

Describe/Draw: The shape is a rectangle, and we are looking at the perimeter.

height

base

Define		**Do**	**Decide**
Height (trial)	Base (height + 13)	Perimeter 2(base) + 2(height)	58
Trial 1: 10	10 + 13 = 23	2(23) + 2(10) = 66	66 is too high

Use any trial value.

Use the relationships stated in the problem to determine the values of the other quantities (such as base and perimeter).

Now use the trial to create an equation by defining and adding a variable line.

| Let x represent the height in cm | x | $x + 13$ | $2(x) + 2(x + 13)$ | $2(x) + 2(x + 13) = 58$ |

Now use your algebra skills to solve the equation.

Declare: The base is 21 centimeters, and the height is 8 centimeters
If you do not write an equation, you can solve the problem by making more trials until you find the answer.

PROPORTIONAL RELATIONSHIPS

A **proportional relationship** can be seen in a table: if one quantity is multiplied by an amount, the corresponding quantity is multiplied by the same amount. On a graph, a proportional relationship is linear and goes through the origin.

Proportional example: Three pounds of chicken costs $7.00. Below, other values are shown in the table and plotted on the graph.

Pounds	0	3	6	9	12
Cost ($)	0	7	14	21	28

The relationship between pounds and cost is proportional.

Games	0	1	2	3	4
Cost ($)	5	6	7	8	9

Non-proportional example: The video arcade costs $5.00 to enter and $1.00 per game.

The relationship between games and cost is *not* proportional. For example, someone who plays four games ($9) does not pay twice as much as someone who played two games ($7). There is no multiplier for the relationship. The graph does not go through the origin.

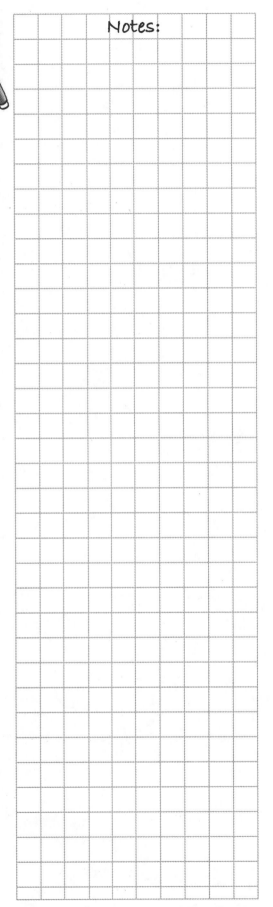

Notes:

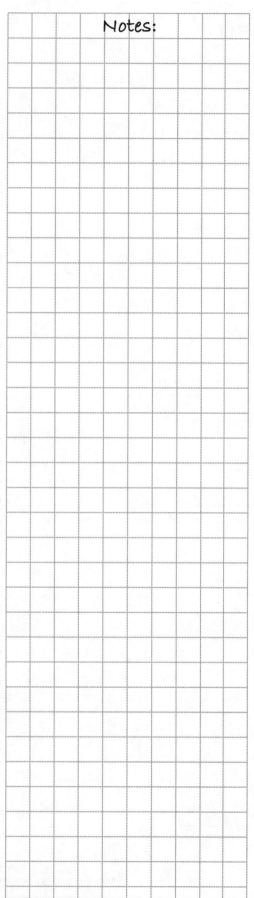

Notes:

SOLVING PROPORTIONS

If a relationship is known to be proportional, ratios from the situation are equal. An equation stating that two ratios are equal is called a **proportion**. Some examples of proportions are:

$$\frac{5}{7} = \frac{50}{70} \qquad\qquad \frac{6\text{ mi}}{2\text{ hr}} = \frac{9\text{ mi}}{3\text{ hr}}$$

Setting up a proportion is one strategy for solving for an unknown part of one ratio. For example, if the ratios $\frac{9}{2}$ and $\frac{x}{16}$ are equal, setting up the proportion $\frac{x}{16} = \frac{9}{2}$ allows you to solve for x.

Giant One: One way to solve this proportion is by using a Giant One to find the equivalent ratio. In this case, since 16 is 2 times 8, you create the Giant One shown at right.

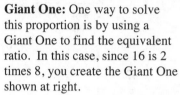

$$\frac{x}{16} = \frac{9}{2} \cdot \boxed{\frac{8}{8}}$$

$$\frac{x}{16} = \frac{9 \cdot 8}{2 \cdot 8}$$

$$\frac{x}{16} = \frac{72}{16}$$

which shows that $x = 72$.

Undoing Division: Another way to solve the proportion is to think of the ratio $\frac{x}{16}$ as, "x divided by 16." To solve for x, use the inverse operation of division, which is multiplication. Multiplying both sides of the proportional equation by 16 "undoes" the division.

$$\frac{x}{16} = \frac{9}{2}$$

$$\left(\frac{16}{1}\right)\frac{x}{16} = \frac{9}{2}\left(\frac{16}{1}\right)$$

$$x = \frac{144}{2}$$

$$x = 72$$

Cross-Multiplication: This method of solving the proportion is a shortcut for using a Fraction Buster (multiplying each side of the equation by the denominators).

Fraction Buster	Cross-Multiplication
$\frac{x}{16} = \frac{9}{2}$	$\frac{x}{16} = \frac{9}{2}$
$2 \cdot 16 \cdot \frac{x}{16} = \frac{9}{2} \cdot 2 \cdot 16$	$\frac{x}{16} \diagdown\!\!\!\!\diagup \frac{9}{2}$
$2 \cdot x = 9 \cdot 16$	$2 \cdot x = 9 \cdot 16$
$2x = 144$	$2x = 144$
$x = 72$	$x = 72$

CHAPTER 2: SIMPLIFYING WITH VARIABLES

Date: Lesson:	Learning Log Title:

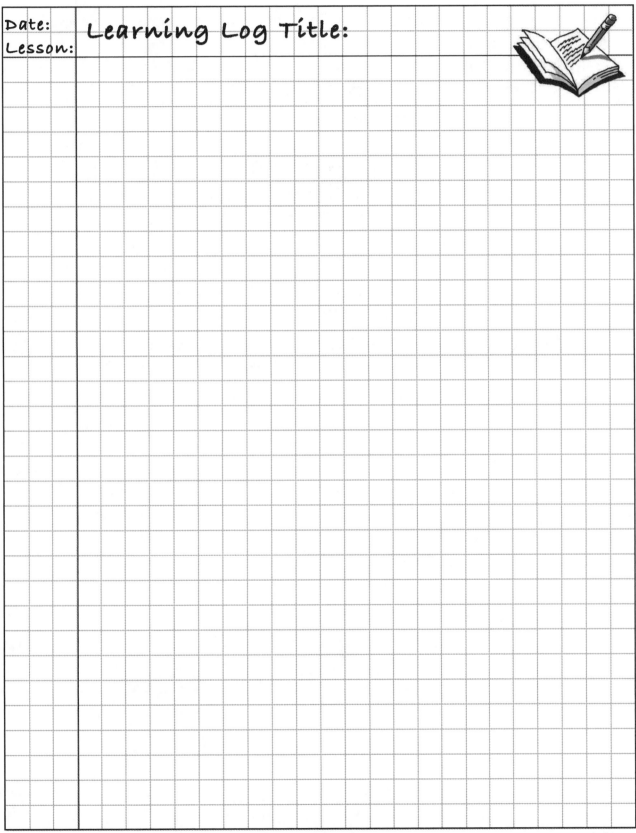

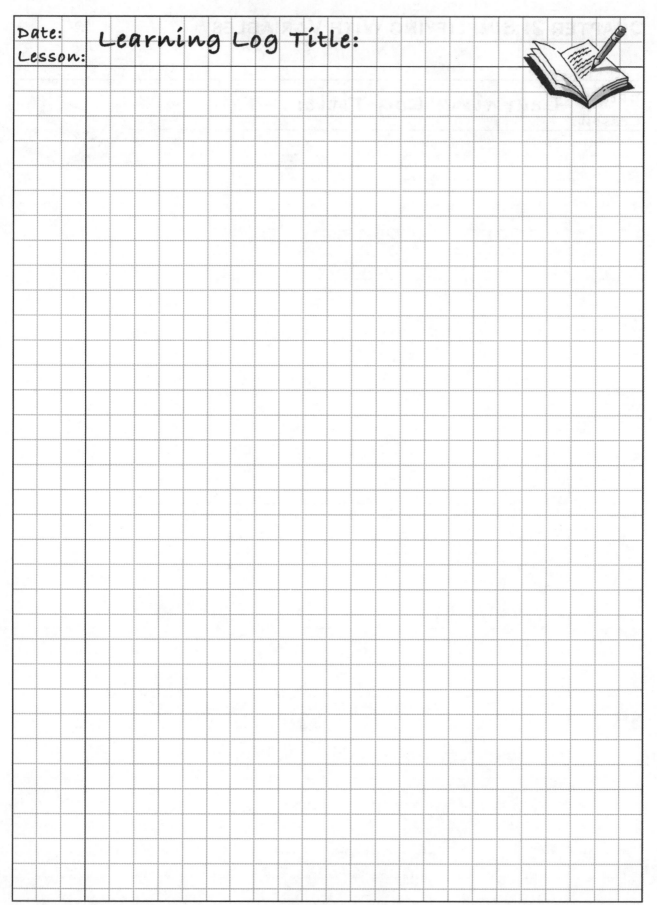

Date:	Learning Log Title:
Lesson:	

Date: Lesson:	Learning Log Title:

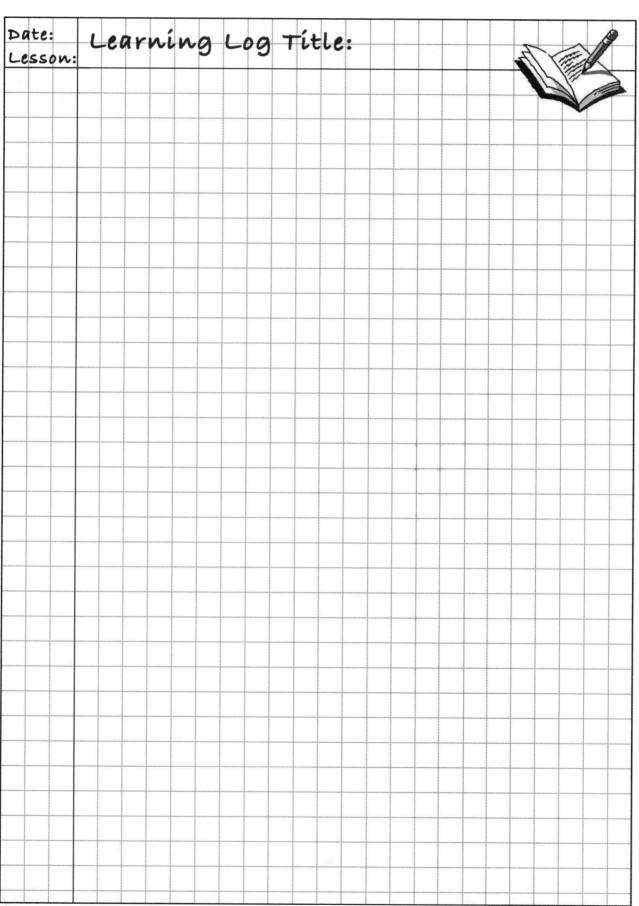

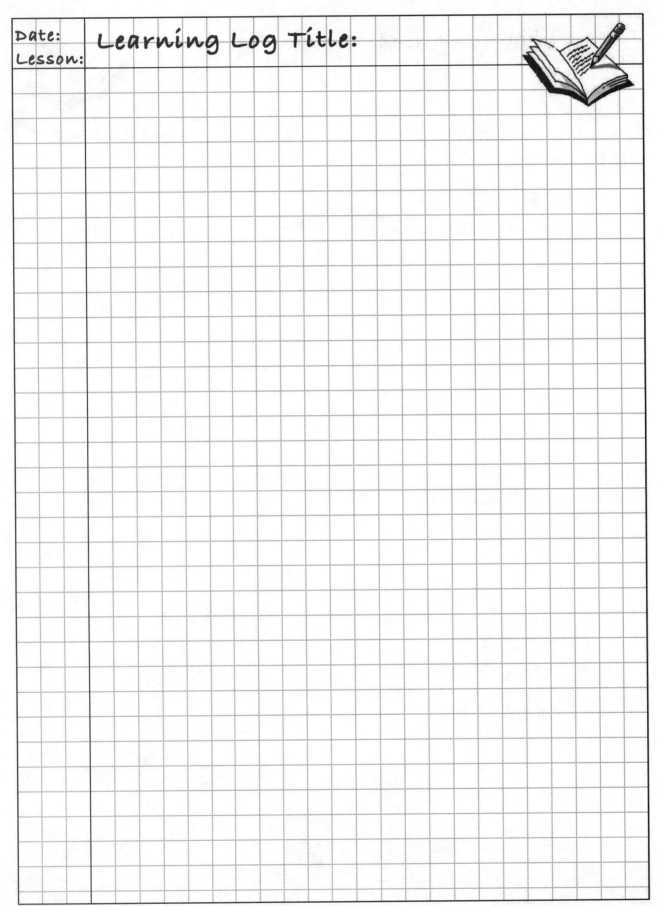

Date:	Learning Log Title:
Lesson:	

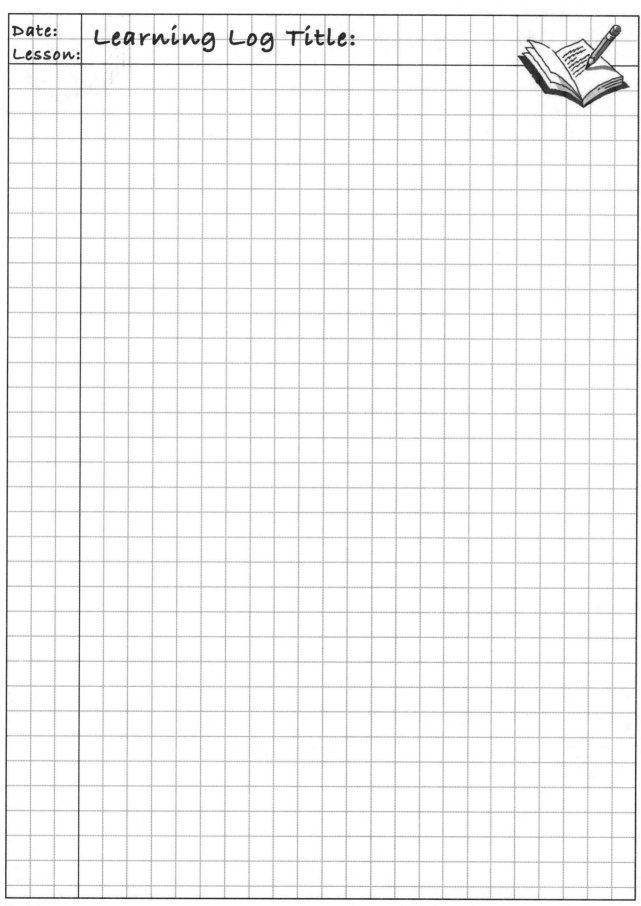

Date: Lesson:	Learning Log Title:

Date: Lesson:	Learning Log Title:	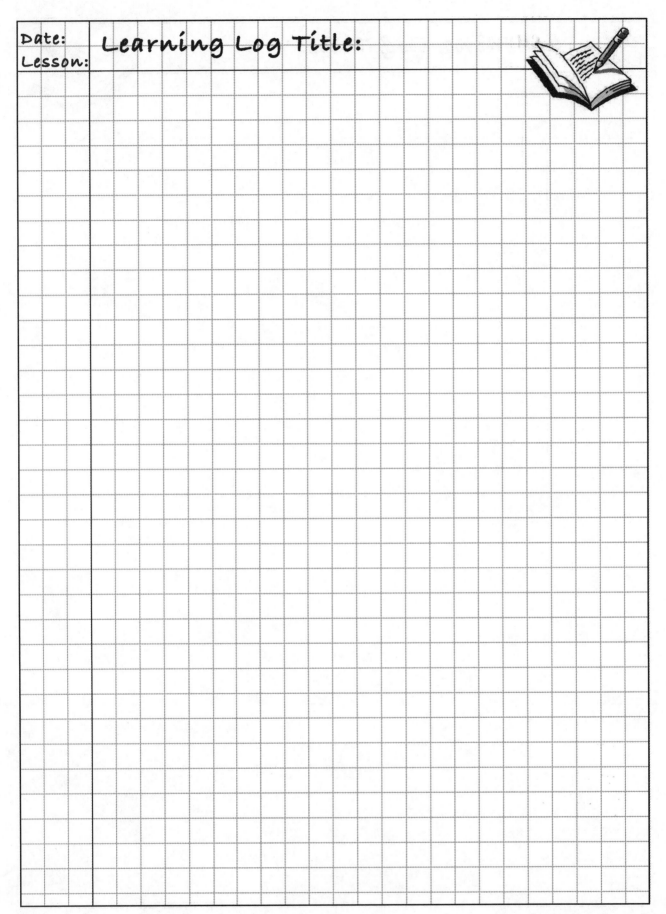

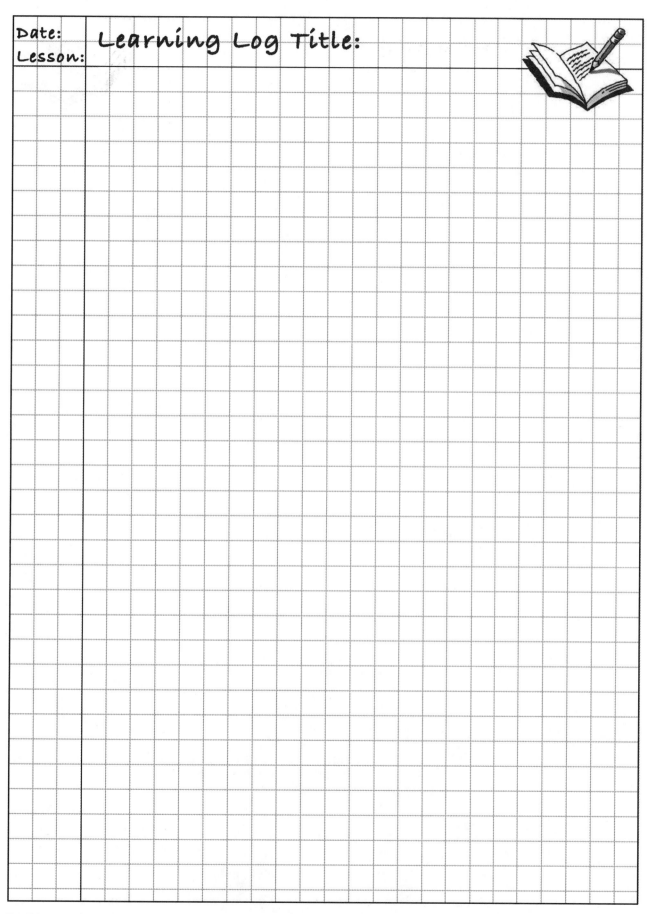

Date:

Lesson:

Learning Log Title:

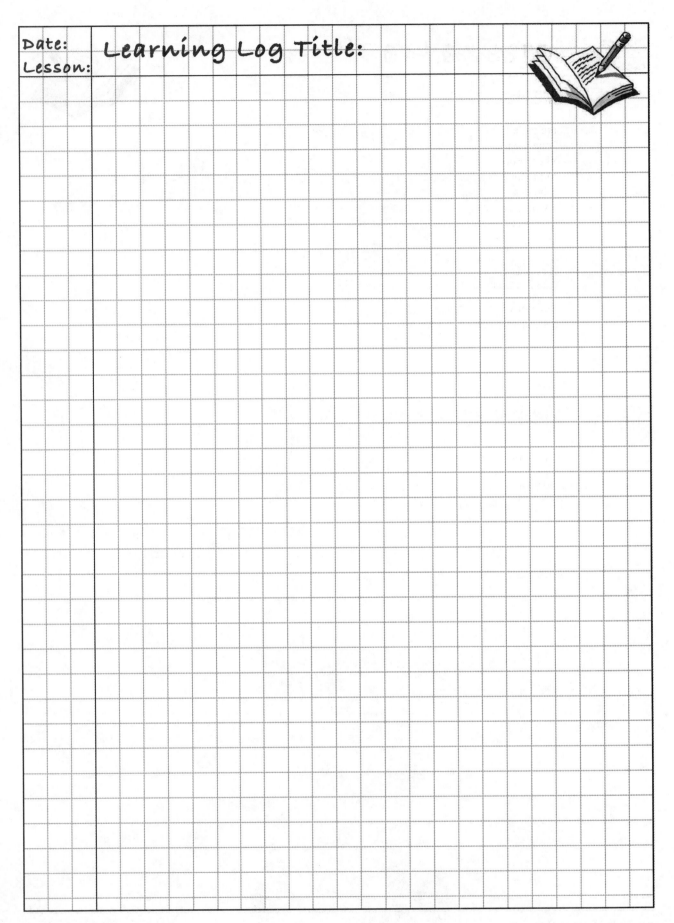

Date:
Lesson:

Learning Log Title:

MATH NOTES

NON-COMMENSURATE

Two measurements are called **non-commensurate** if no combination of one measurement can equal a combination of the other. For example, your algebra tiles are called non-commensurate because no combination of unit squares will ever be exactly equal to a combination of x-tiles (although at times they may appear close in comparison). In the same way, in the example below, no combination of x-tiles will ever be exactly equal to a combination of y-tiles.

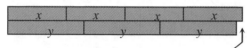

No matter what number of each size tile, these two piles will never exactly

MATHEMATICS VOCABULARY

Variable: A letter or symbol that represents one or more numbers.

Expression: A combination of numbers, variables, and operation symbols. For example, $2x + 3(5 - 2x) + 8$. Also, $5 - 2x$ is a smaller expression within the larger expression.

Term: Parts of the expression separated by addition and subtraction. For example, in the expression $2x + 3(5 - 2x) + 8$, the three terms are $2x$, $3(5 - 2x)$, and 8. The expression $5 - 2x$ has two terms, 5 and $-2x$.

Coefficient: The numerical part of a term. In the expression $2x + 3(5 - 2x) + 8$, for example, 2 is the coefficient of $2x$. In the expression $7x - 15x^2$, both 7 and 15 are coefficients.

Constant term: A number that is not multiplied by a variable. In the expression $2x + 3(5 - 2x) + 8$, the number 8 is a constant term. The number 3 is not a constant term, because it is multiplied by a variable inside the parentheses.

Factor: Part of a multiplication expression. In the expression $3(5 - 2x)$, 3 and $5 - 2x$ are factors.

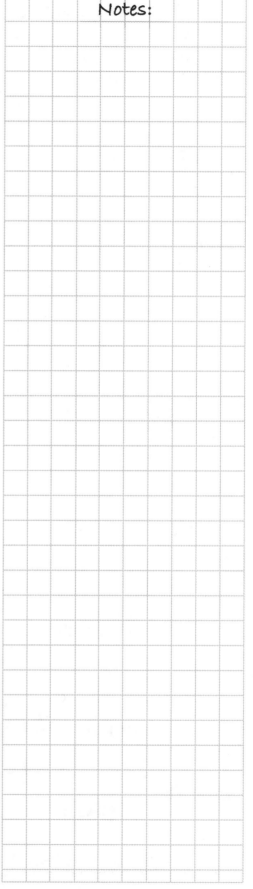

Notes:

COMBINING LIKE TERMS

Combining tiles that have the same area to write a simpler expression is called **combining like terms**. See the example shown at right.

When you are not working with actual tiles, it can help to picture the tiles in your mind. You can use these images to combine the terms that are the same. Here are two examples:

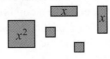

$$x^2 + 2x + 2$$

Example 1:

$$2x^2 + xy + y^2 + x + 3 + x^2 + 3xy + 2 \Rightarrow 3x^2 + 4xy + y^2 + x + 5$$

Example 2:

$$3x^2 - 2x + 7 - 5x^2 + 3x - 2 \Rightarrow -2x^2 + x + 5$$

A **term** is an algebraic expression that is a single number, a single variable, or the product of numbers and variables. The simplified algebraic expression in Example 2 above contains three terms. The first term is $-2x^2$, the second term is x, and the third term is 5.

EVALUATING EXPRESSIONS AND THE ORDER OF OPERATIONS

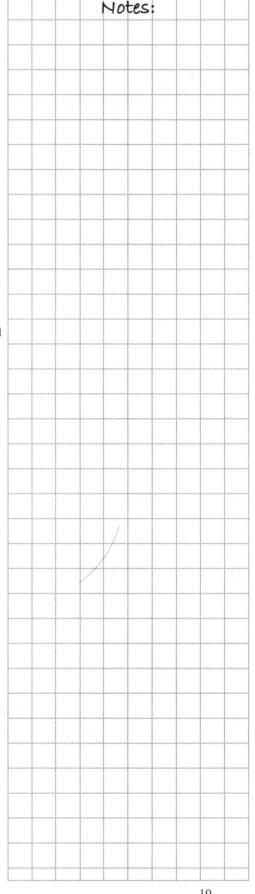

To **evaluate** an algebraic expression for particular values of the variables, replace the variables in the expression with their known numerical values and simplify. Replacing variables with their known values is called **substitution**. An example is provided below.

Evaluate $4x - 3y + 7$ for $x = 2$ and $y = 1$.

Replace x and y with their known values of 2 and 1, respectively, and simplify.

$$4(2) - 3(1) + 7$$
$$= 8 - 3 + 7$$
$$= 12$$

When evaluating a complex expression, you must remember to use the **Order of Operations** that mathematicians have agreed upon. As illustrated in the example below, the order of operations is:

Original expression:

$$(10 - 3 \cdot 2) \cdot 2^2 - \frac{13 - 3^2}{2} + 6$$

Circle expressions that are grouped within parentheses or by a fraction bar:

$$\boxed{(10 - 3 \cdot 2)} \cdot 2^2 - \boxed{\frac{13 - 3^2}{2}} + 6$$

Simplify *within* circled terms using the order of operations:

$$\boxed{(10 - 3 \cdot 2)} \cdot 2^2 - \boxed{\frac{13 - 3 \cdot 3}{2}} + 6$$

- Evaluate exponents.

$$\boxed{(10 - 6)} \cdot 2^2 - \boxed{\frac{13 - 9}{2}} + 6$$

- Multiply and divide from left to right.

$$(4) \cdot 2^2 - \frac{4}{2} + 6$$

- Combine terms by adding and subtracting from left to right.

$$\boxed{4 \cdot 2^2} - \boxed{\frac{4}{2}} + \boxed{6}$$

Circle the remaining terms:

$$\boxed{4 \cdot 2 \cdot 2} - \boxed{\frac{4}{2}} + \boxed{6}$$

$$16 - 2 + 6$$

Simplify *within* circled terms using the Order of Operations as described above.

$$20$$

Notes:

COMMUTATIVE PROPERTIES

The **Commutative Property of Addition** states that when *adding* two or more number or terms together, order is not important. That is:

$$a + b = b + a .$$ For example, $2 + 7 = 7 + 2$

The **Commutative Property of Multiplication** states that when *multiplying* two or more numbers or terms together, order is not important. That is:

$$a \cdot b = b \cdot a .$$ For example, $3 \cdot 5 = 5 \cdot 3$

However, *subtraction* and *division* are not commutative, as shown below.

$$7 - 2 \neq 2 - 7 \text{ since } 5 \neq -5$$

$$50 \div 10 \neq 10 \div 50 \text{ since } 5 \neq 0.2$$

SIMPLIFYING AN EXPRESSION ("LEGAL MOVES")

Three common ways to simplify or alter expressions on an Expression Mat are illustrated below.

- Removing an equal number of opposite tiles that are in the same region. For example, the positive and negative tiles in the same region at right combine to make zero.

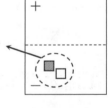

- Flipping a tile to move it out of one region into the opposite region (i.e., finding its opposite). For example, the tiles in the "–" region at right can be flipped into the "+" region.

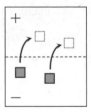

- Removing an equal number of identical tiles from both the "–" and the "+" regions. This strategy can be seen as a combination of the two methods above, since you could first flip the tiles from one region to another and then remove the opposite pairs.

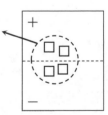

ASSOCIATIVE AND IDENTITY PROPERTIES

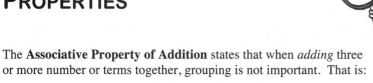

The **Associative Property of Addition** states that when *adding* three or more number or terms together, grouping is not important. That is:

$$(a+b)+c = a+(b+c)$$ For example, $(5+2)+6 = 5+(2+6)$

The **Associative Property of Multiplication** states that when *multiplying* three or more numbers or terms together, grouping is not important. That is:

$$(a \cdot b) \cdot c = a \cdot (b \cdot c)$$ For example, $(5 \cdot 2) \cdot 6 = 5 \cdot (2 \cdot 6)$

However, *subtraction* and *division* are not associative, as shown below.

$$(5-2)-3 \neq 5-(2-3) \text{ since } 0 \neq 6$$

$$(20 \div 4) \div 2 \neq 20 \div (4 \div 2) \text{ since } 2.5 \neq 10$$

The **Identity Property of Addition** states that adding zero to any expression gives the same expression. That is:

$$a+0 = a$$ For example, $6+0 = 6$

The **Identity Property of Multiplication** states that multiplying any expression by one gives the same expression. That is:

$$1 \cdot a = a$$ For example, $1 \cdot 6 = 6$

INVERSE PROPERTIES

The **Additive Inverse Property** states that for every number a there is a number $-a$ such that $a+(-a) = 0$. A common name used for the additive inverse is the **opposite**. That is, $-a$ is the opposite of a. For example, $3+(-3) = 0$ and $-5+5 = 0$.

The **Multiplicative Inverse Property** states that for every nonzero number a there is a number $\frac{1}{a}$ such that $a \cdot \frac{1}{a} = 1$ A common name used for the multiplicative inverse is the **reciprocal**. That is, $\frac{1}{a}$ is the reciprocal of a. For example, $6 \cdot \frac{1}{6} = 1$.

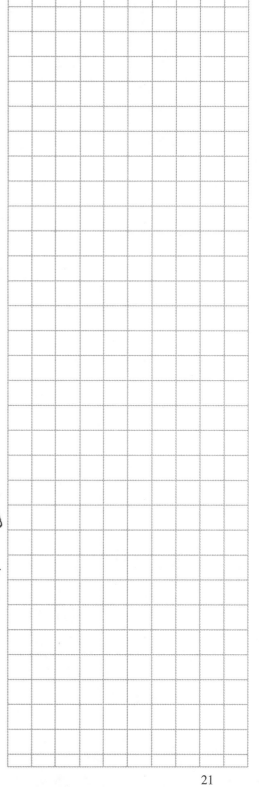

Notes:

USING AN EQUATION MAT

An **Equation Mat** can help
you visually represent an
equation with algebra tiles.

The double line
represents the "equal"
sign (=).

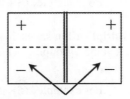

For each side of the equation,
there is a positive and a
negative region.

For example, the equation $2x - 1 - (-x + 3) = 6 - 2x$ can be represented by
the Equation Mat at right. (Note that there are other possible ways to
represent this equation correctly on the Equation Mat.)

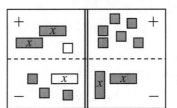

 = +1
□ = −1

CHAPTER 3: GRAPHS AND EQUATIONS

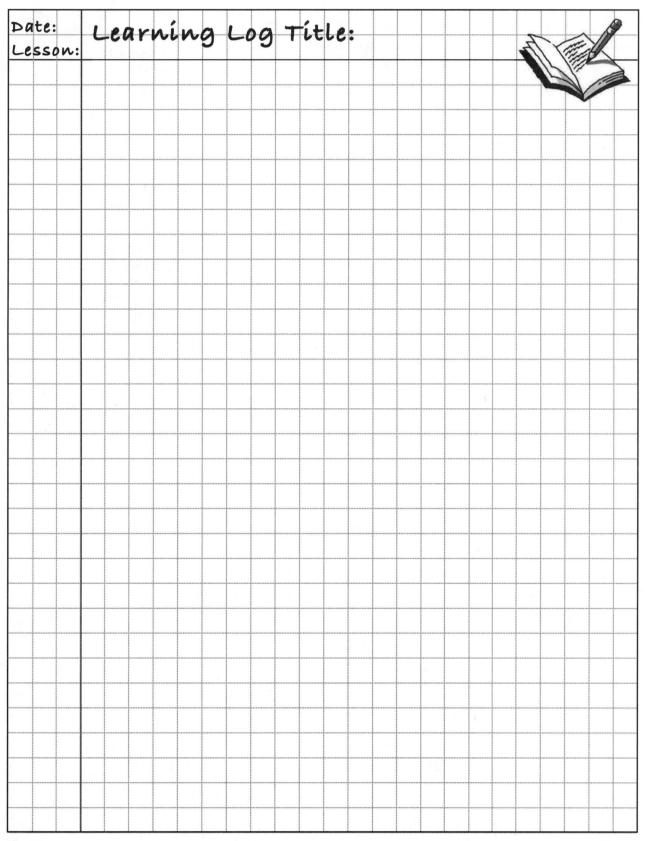

Date: Lesson:	Learning Log Title:

Date:	Learning Log Title:
Lesson:	

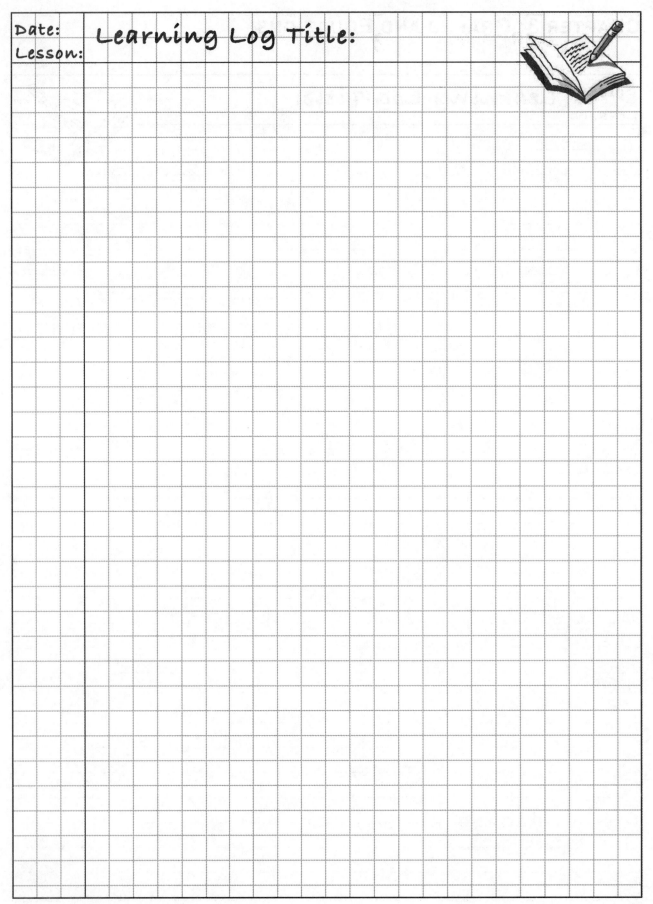

Date:	Learning Log Title:
Lesson:	

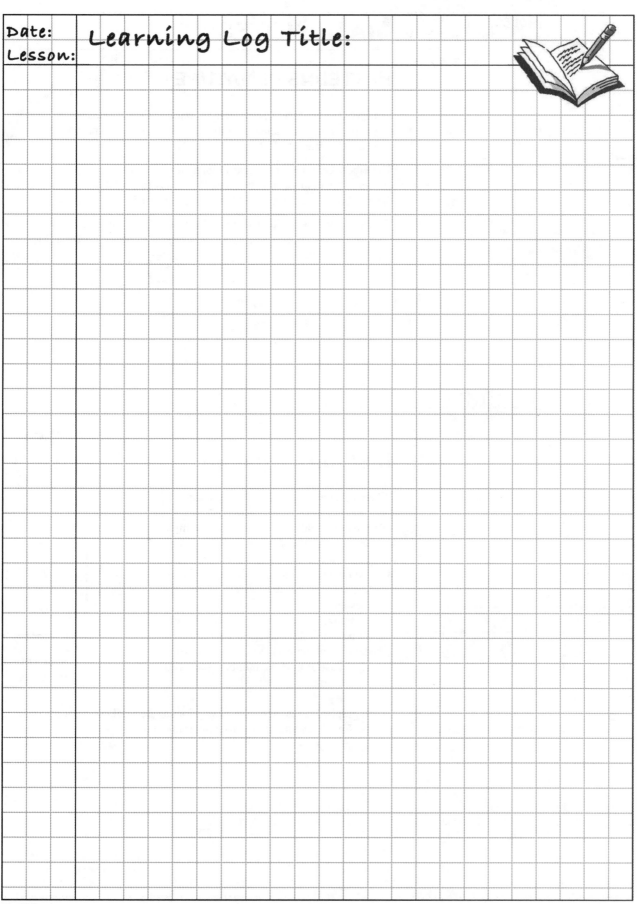

MATH NOTES

PATTERNS IN NATURE

Patterns are everywhere, especially in nature. One famous pattern that appears often is called the Fibonacci Sequence, a sequence of numbers that starts 1, 1, 2, 3, 5, 8, 13, 21, …

The Fibonacci numbers appear in many different situations in nature. For example, the number of petals on a flower is often a Fibonacci number, and the number of seeds on a spiral from the center of a sunflower is, too.

To learn more about Fibonacci numbers, search the Internet or check out a book from your local library. The next time you look at a flower, look for Fibonacci numbers!

DISCRETE GRAPHS

When a graph of data is limited to a set of separate, non-connected points, that relationship is called **discrete**. For example, consider the relationship between the number of bicycles parked at your school and the number of bicycle wheels. If there is one bicycle, it has two wheels. Two bicycles have four wheels, while three bicycles have six wheels. However, there cannot be 1.3 or 2.9 bicycles. Therefore, this data is limited because the number of bicycles must be a whole number, such as 0, 1, 2, 3, and so on.

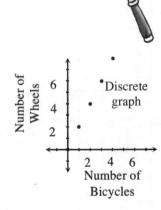

When graphed, a discrete relationship looks like a collection of unconnected points. See the example of a discrete graph above.

CONTINUOUS GRAPHS

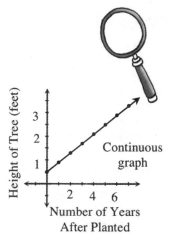

When a set of data is not confined to separate points and instead consists of connected points, the data is called **continuous**. "John's Giant Redwood," problem 3-11, is an example of a continuous situation, because even though the table focuses on integer values of years (1, 2, 3, etc.), the tree still grows between these values of time. Therefore, the tree has a height at any non-negative value of time (such as 1.1 years after it is planted).

When data for a continuous relationship are graphed, the points are connected to show that the relationship also holds true for all points between the table values. See the example of a continuous graph above.

Note: In this course, tile patterns will represent elements of continuous relationships and will be graphed with a continuous line or curve.

PARABOLAS

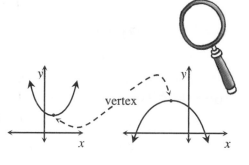

One kind of graph you will study in this class is called a **parabola**. Two examples of parabolas are graphed at right. Note that parabolas are smooth "U" shapes, not pointy "V" shapes.

The point where a parabola turns (the highest or lowest point) is called the **vertex**.

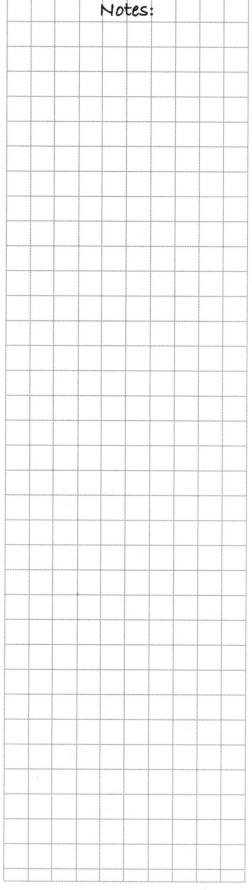

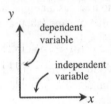

INDEPENDENT AND DEPENDENT VARIABLES

When one quantity (such as the height of a redwood tree) depends on another (such as the number of years after the tree was planted), it is called a **dependent variable**. That means its value is determined by the value of another variable. The dependent variable is usually graphed on the y-axis.

If a quantity, such as time, does not depend on another variable, it is referred to as the **independent variable**, which is graphed on the x-axis.

For example, in problem 3-46, you compared the amount of a dinner bill with the amount of a tip. In this case, the tip depends on the amount of the dinner bill. Therefore, the tip is the dependent variable, while the dinner bill is the independent variable.

COMPLETE GRAPH

A complete graph has the following components:

- x-axis and y-axis labeled, clearly showing the scale.

- Equation of the graph near the line or curve.

- Line or curve extended as far as possible on the graph.

Coordinates of special points stated in (x, y) format.

Tables can be formatted horizontally, like the one at right, or vertically, as shown below.

x	-1	0	1	2	3	4
y	6	4	2	0	-2	-4

x	y
-1	6
0	4
1	2
2	0
3	-2
4	-4

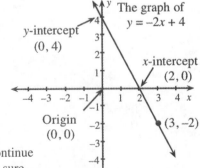

Throughout this course, you will continue to graph lines and other curves. Be sure to label your graphs appropriately.

Notes:

CIRCULAR VOCABULARY, CIRCUMFERENCE, AND AREA

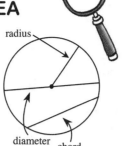

The **radius** of a circle is a line segment from its center to any point on the circle. The term is also used for the length of these segments. More than one radius are called **radii**.

A **chord** of a circle is a line segment joining any two points on a circle.

A **diameter** of a circle is a chord that goes through its center. The term is also used for the length of these chords. The length of a diameter is twice the length of a radius.

The **circumference** (C) of a circle is its perimeter, or the "distance around" the circle.

$$C = \pi \cdot d$$

The number π (read "pi") is the ratio of the circumference of a circle to its diameter. That is, $\pi = \frac{\text{circumference}}{\text{diameter}}$. This definition is also used as a way of computing the circumference of a circle if you know the diameter, as in the formula $C = \pi d$ where C is the circumference and d is the diameter. Since the diameter is twice the radius ($d = 2r$), the formula for the circumference of a circle using its radius is $C = \pi(2r)$ or $C = 2\pi \cdot r$.

The first few digits of π are 3.141592.

To find the **area** (A) of a circle when given its radius (r), square the radius and multiply by π. This formula can be written as $A = r^2 \cdot \pi$. Another way the area formula is often written is $A = \pi \cdot r^2$.

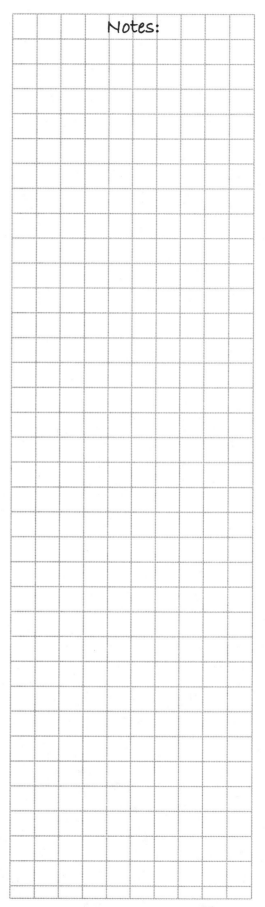

Notes:

Notes:

SOLVING A LINEAR EQUATION

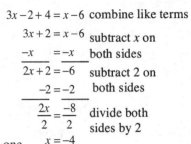

When solving an equation like the one shown below, several important strategies are involved.

- **Simplify.** Combine like terms and "make zeros" on each side of the equation whenever possible.

- **Keep equations balanced.** The equal sign in an equation indicates that the expressions on the left and right are balanced. Anything done to the equation must keep that balance.

$3x - 2 + 4 = x - 6$ combine like terms

$3x + 2 = x - 6$ subtract x on

$\underline{-x \quad\quad = -x}$ both sides

$2x + 2 = -6$ subtract 2 on

$\underline{\quad -2 = -2}$ both sides

$\dfrac{2x}{2} = \dfrac{-8}{2}$ divide both sides by 2

$x = -4$

- **Get x alone.** Isolate the variable on one side of the equation and the constants on the other.

- **Undo operations.** Use the fact that addition is the opposite of subtraction and that multiplication is the opposite of division to solve for x. For example, in the equation $2x = -8$, since the 2 and x are multiplied, dividing both sides by 2 will get x alone.

SOLUTIONS TO AN EQUATION WITH ONE VARIABLE

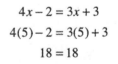

A **solution** to an equation gives a value of the variable that makes the equation true. For example, when 5 is substituted for x in the equation at right, both sides of the equation are equal. So $x = 5$ is a solution to this equation.

$4x - 2 = 3x + 3$

$4(5) - 2 = 3(5) + 3$

$18 = 18$

An equation can have more than one solution, or it may have no solution. Consider the examples at right.

Notice that no matter what the value of x is, the left side of the first equation will never equal the right side. Therefore, you say that $x + 2 = x + 6$ has **no solution**.

Equation with no solution:

$x + 2 = x + 6$

However, in the equation $x - 3 = x - 3$, no matter what value x has, the equation will always be true. All numbers can make $x - 3 = x - 3$ true. Therefore, you say the solution for the equation $x - 3 = x - 3$ is **all numbers**.

Equation with infinite solutions:

$x - 3 = x - 3$

THE DISTRIBUTIVE PROPERTY

The **Distributive Property** states that for any three terms a, b, and c:

$$a(b + c) = ab + ac$$

That is, when a multiplies a group of terms, such as $(b + c)$, it multiplies *each* term of the group. For example, when multiplying $2(x + 4)$, the 2 multiplies both the x and the 4. This can be represented with algebra tiles, as shown below.

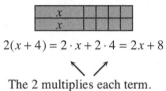

$$2(x + 4) = 2 \cdot x + 2 \cdot 4 = 2x + 8$$

The 2 multiplies each term.

Notes:

CHAPTER 4: MULTIPLE REPRESENTATIONS

Date: Lesson:	Learning Log Title:

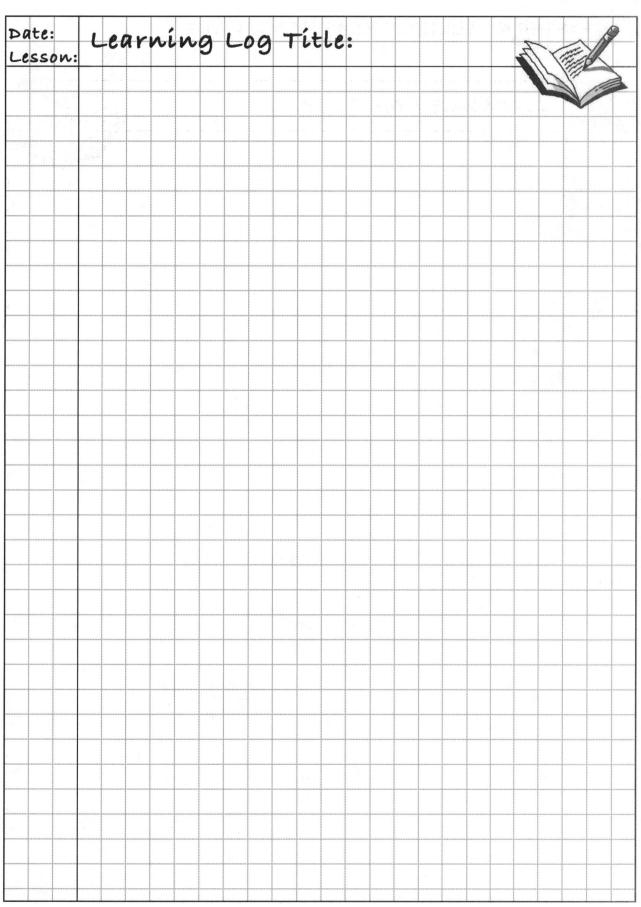

Date: Lesson:	Learning Log Title:

Date:	Learning Log Title:
Lesson:	

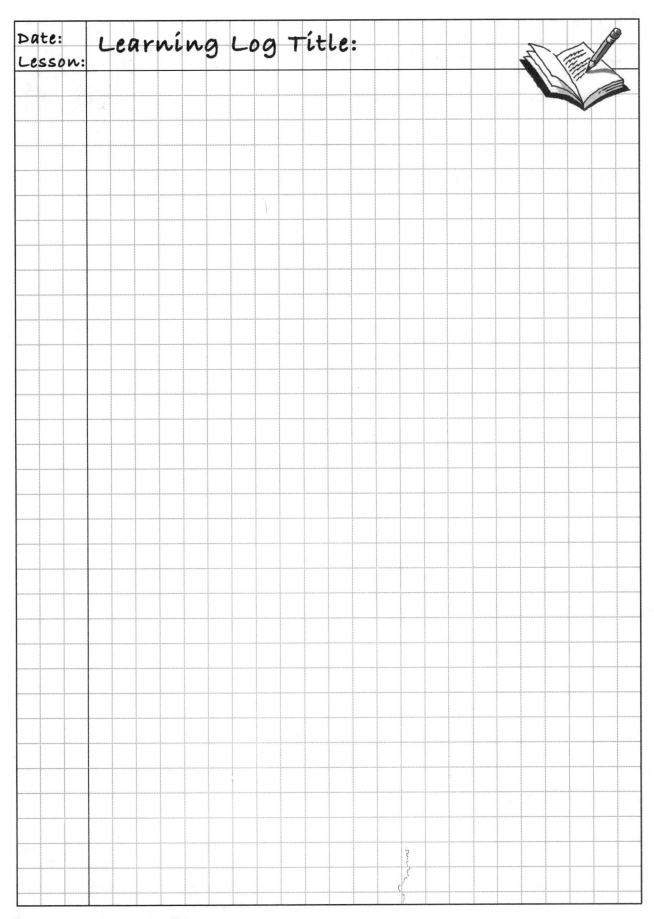

Date:	Learning Log Title:
Lesson:	

Date:	Learning Log Title:
Lesson:	

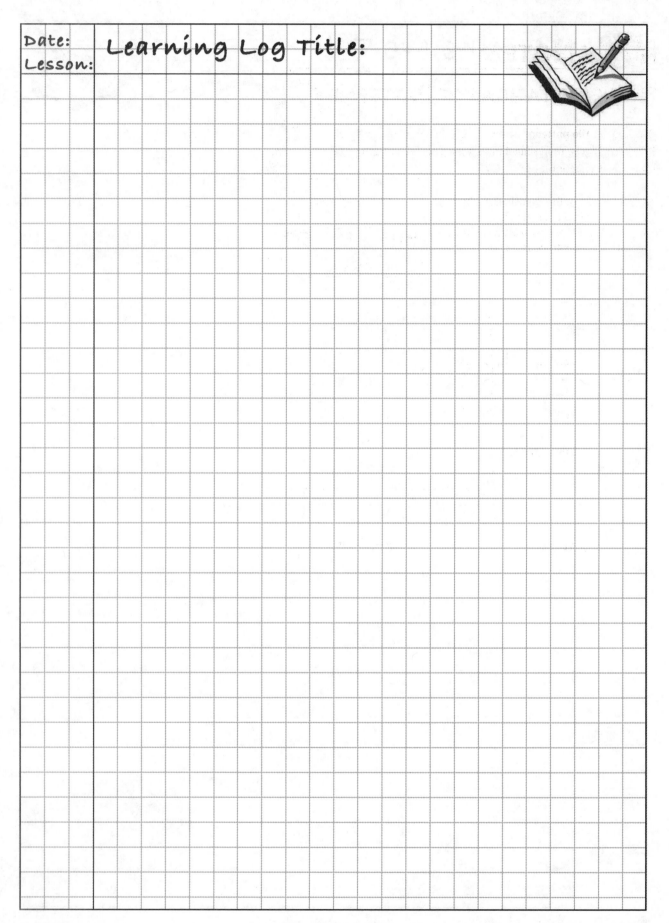

MATH NOTES

REPRESENTATIONS OF PATTERNS

Consider the **tile patterns** below. The number of tiles in each figure can also be represented in an $x \rightarrow y$ **table**, on a **graph**, or with a **rule** (equation).

Remember that in this course, tile patterns will be considered to be elements of continuous relationships and thus will be graphed with a continuous line or curve.

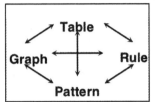

Table

Graph ←→ Rule

Pattern

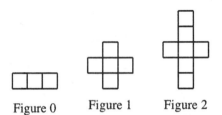

Figure 0   Figure 1   Figure 2

Tile Pattern

Graph

$$y = 2x + 3$$

Figure Number (x)	0	1	2
Number of Tiles (y)	3	5	7

Rule (Equation) $x \rightarrow y$ **Table**

Date: Lesson:	Learning Log Title:

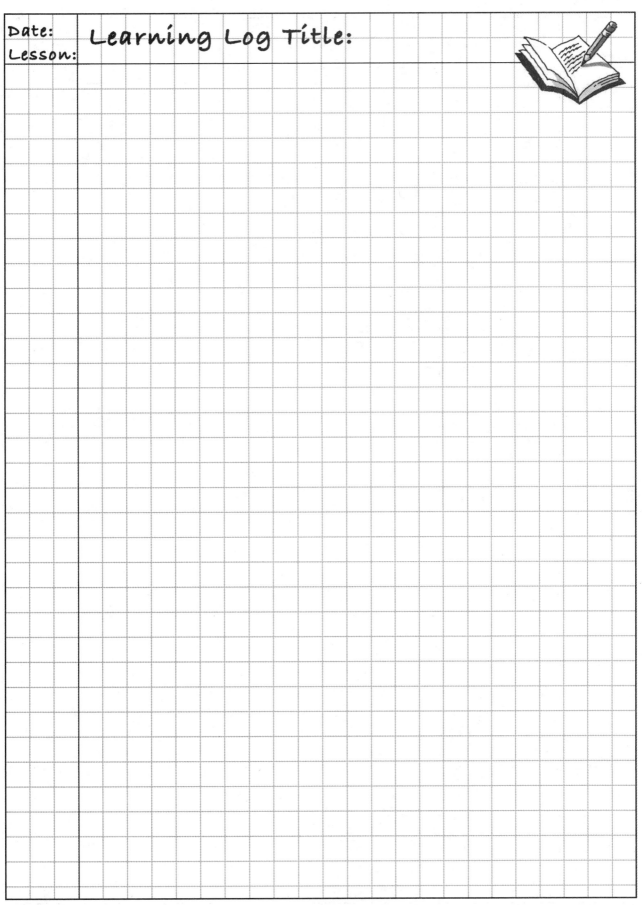

Date:
Lesson:

Learning Log Title:

Date:	Learning Log Title:
Lesson:	

MATH NOTES

LINEAR EQUATIONS

A **linear equation** is an equation that forms a line when it is graphed. This type of equation may be written in several different forms. Although these forms look different, they are equivalent; that is, they all graph the same line.

Standard form: An equation in $ax + by = c$ form, such as $-6x + 3y = 18$.

$y = mx + b$ **form:** An equation in $y = mx + b$ form, such as $y = 2x + 6$.

You can quickly find the **growth factor** and **y-intercept** of a line in $y = mx + b$ form. For the equation $y = 2x - 6$, the growth factor is 2, while the y-intercept is $(0, -6)$.

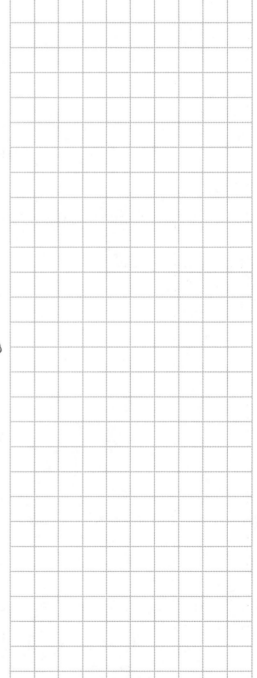

y-intercept — *growth factor*

$$y = 2x - 6$$

growth factor   *y-intercept*

EQUIVALENT EQUATIONS

Two equations are **equivalent** if they have all the same solutions. There are many ways to change one equation into a different, equivalent equation. Common ways include: *adding* the same number to both sides, *subtracting* the same number from both sides, *multiplying* both sides by the same number, *dividing* both sides by the same (non-zero) number, and *rewriting* one or both sides of the equation.

For example, the equations below are all equivalent to $2x + 1 = 3$:

$$20x + 10 = 30 \qquad\qquad 2(x + 0.5) = 3$$

$$\frac{2x}{3} + \frac{1}{3} = 1 \qquad\qquad 0.002x + 0.001 = 0.003$$

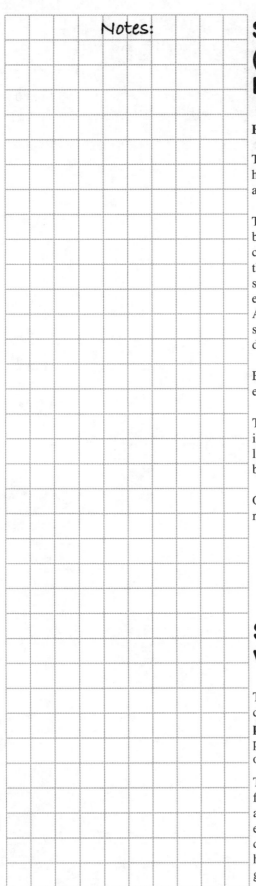

Notes:

Solving Equations with Fractions (also Known as the Fraction Buster Method)

Example: Solve $\frac{x}{3} + \frac{x}{5} = 2$ for x.

This equation would be much easier to solve if it had no fractions. Therefore, the first goal is to find an equivalent equation that has no fractions.

$$\frac{x}{3} + \frac{x}{5} = 2$$

To eliminate the denominators, multiply both sides of the equation by the common denominator. In this example, the lowest common denominator is 15, so multiplying both sides of the equation by 15 eliminates the fractions. Another approach is to multiply both sides of the equation by one denominator and then by the other.

The lowest common denominator of $\frac{x}{3}$ and $\frac{x}{5}$ is 15.

$$15 \cdot \left(\frac{x}{3} + \frac{x}{5} \right) = 15 \cdot 2$$

$$15 \cdot \frac{x}{3} + 15 \cdot \frac{x}{5} = 15 \cdot 2$$

Either way, the result is an equivalent equation without fractions:

$$5x + 3x = 30$$
$$8x = 30$$

The number used to eliminate the denominators is called a **Fraction Buster**. Now the equation looks like many you have seen before, and it can be solved in the usual way.

$$x = \frac{30}{8} = \frac{15}{4} = 3.75$$

Once you have found the solution, remember to check your answer.

$$\frac{3.75}{3} + \frac{3.75}{5} = 2$$

$$1.25 + 0.75 = 2$$

System of Equations Vocabulary

The point where two lines or curves intersect is called a **point of intersection**. This point's significance depends on the context of the problem.

Two or more lines or curves used to find a point of intersection are called a **system of equations**. A system of equations can represent a variety of contexts and can be used to compare how two or more things are related. For example, the system of equations graphed above compares the temperature in two different cities over time.

THE EQUAL VALUES METHOD

The **Equal Values Method** is a non-graphing method to find the point of intersection or solution to a system of equations.

Start with two equations in $y = mx + b$ form, such as $y = -2x + 5$ and $y = x - 1$. Take the two expressions that equal y and set them equal to each other. Then solve this new equation to find x. See the example at right.

$$-2x + 5 = x - 1$$
$$-3x = -6$$
$$x = 2$$

Once you know the x-coordinate of the point of intersection, substitute your solution for x into *either* original equation to find y. In this example, the first equation is used.

$$y = -2x + 5$$
$$y = -2(2) + 5$$
$$y = 1$$

A good way to check your solution is to substitute your solution for x into *both* equations to verify that you get equal y-values.

$$y = x - 1$$
$$y = (2) - 1$$
$$y = 1$$

Write the solution as an ordered pair to represent the point on the graph where the equations intersect.

$$(2, 1)$$

SOLUTIONS TO A SYSTEM OF EQUATIONS

A **solution** to a system of equations gives a value for each variable that makes both equations true. For example, when 4 is substituted for x and 5 is substituted for y in both equations at right, both equations are true. So $x = 4$ and $y = 5$ or $(4, 5)$ is a solution to this system of equations. When the two equations are graphed, $(4, 5)$ is the point of intersection.

System with one solution: intersecting lines
$$x - y = -1$$
$$2x - y = 3$$

Some systems of equations have no solutions or infinite solutions. Consider the examples at right.

System with no solution: parallel lines
$$x + y = 3$$
$$x + y = 4$$

Notice that the Equal Values Method would yield $3 = 4$, which is never true. When the lines are graphed, they are parallel. Therefore, the system has **no solution**.

System with infinite solutions: coinciding lines
$$x + y = 3$$
$$2x + 2y = 6$$

In the third set of equations, the second equation is just the first equation multiplied by 2. Therefore, the two lines are really the same line and have **infinite solutions**.

Toolkit

CHAPTER 6: TRANSFORMATIONS AND SIMILARITY

Date: Lesson:	Learning Log Title:

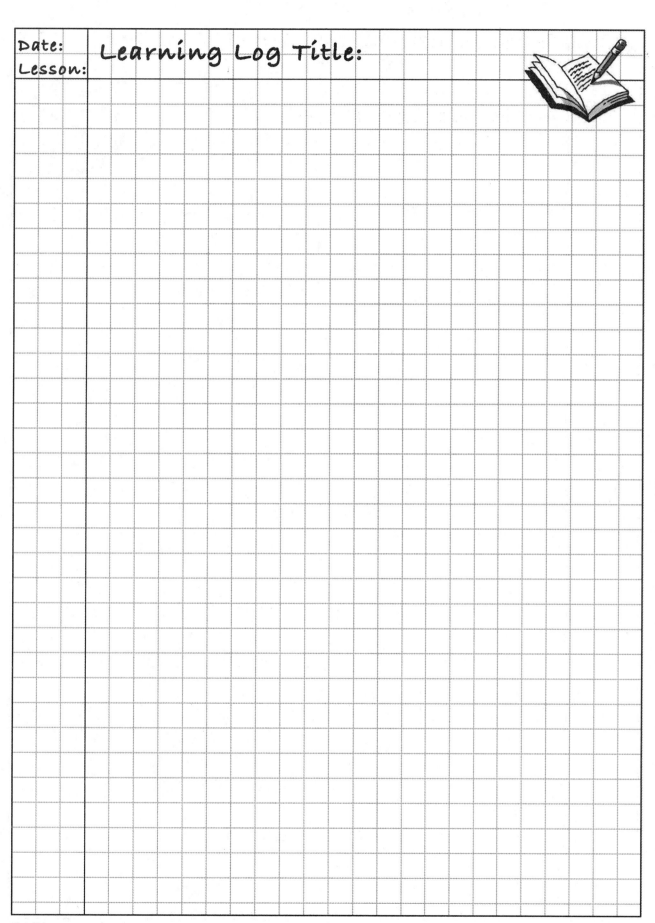

| Date: | Learning Log Title: |
| Lesson: | |

Date:	Learning Log Title:
Lesson:	

Date: Lesson:	Learning Log Title:

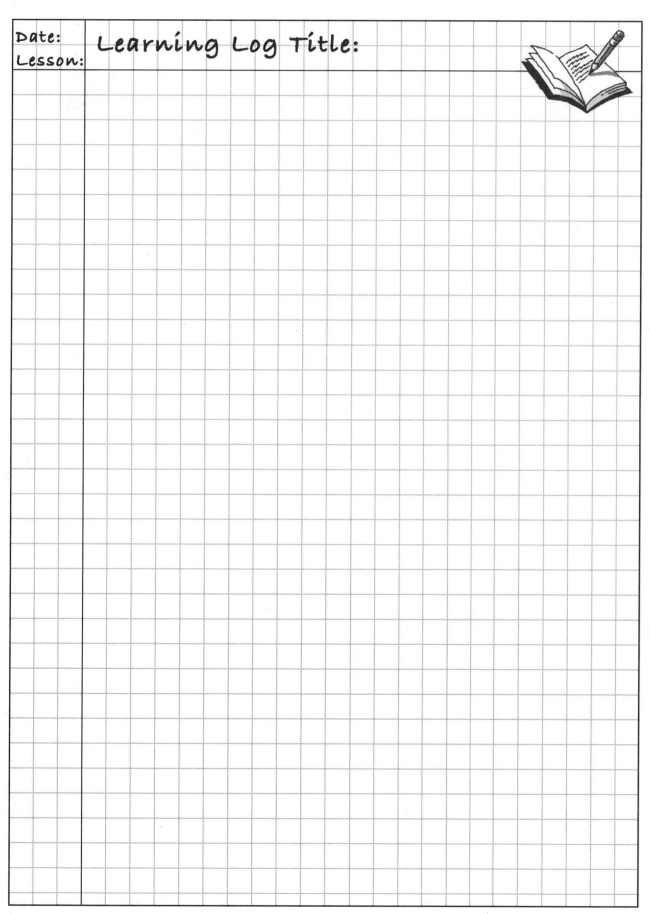

Date: Lesson:	Learning Log Title:	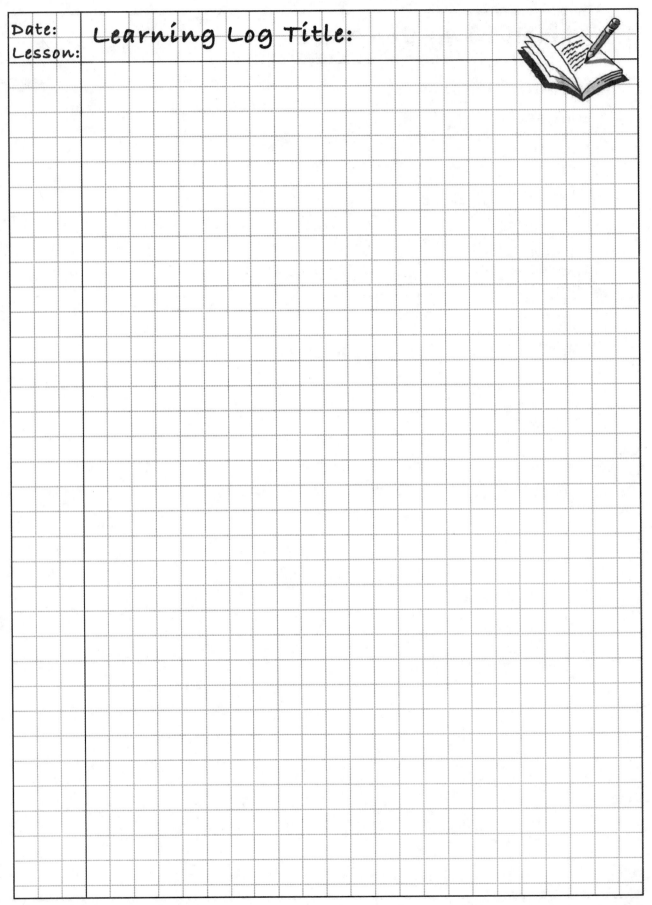

MATH NOTES

RIGID TRANSFORMATIONS

Rigid transformations are ways to move an object while not changing its shape or size. Specifically, they are translations (slides), reflections (flips), and rotations (turns). Each movement is described below.

A **translation** slides an object horizontally (side-to-side), vertically (up or down), or both. To translate an object, you must describe which direction you will move it, and how far it will slide. In the example at right, triangle A is translated 4 units to the right and 3 units up.

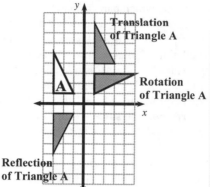

A **reflection** flips an object across a line (called a **line of reflection**). To reflect an object, you must describe the line the object will flip across. In the example at right, triangle A is reflected across the x-axis.

A **rotation** turns an object about a point. To rotate an object, you must choose a point, direction, and angle of rotation. In the example at right, triangle A is rotated 90° clockwise (↻) about the origin $(0,0)$.

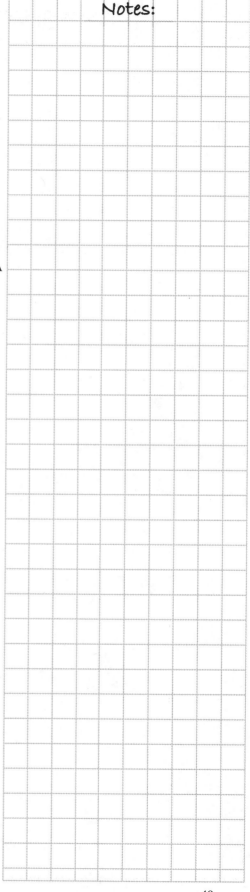

Notes:

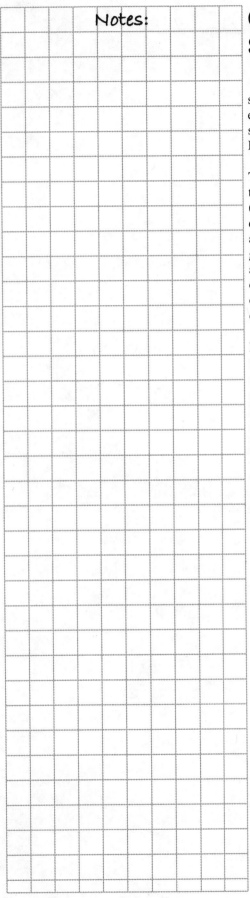

CORRESPONDING PARTS OF SIMILAR SHAPES

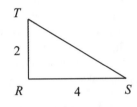

Two figures are **similar** if they have the same shape but not necessarily the same size. For example, all semi-circles are similar, as are all squares, no matter how they are oriented. Dilations create similar figures.

To check whether figures are similar, you need to decide which parts of one figure **correspond** (match up) to which parts of the other. For example, in the triangles at right, triangle *DEF* is a dilation of triangle *ABC*. Side *AB* is dilated to get side *DE*, side *AC* is dilated to get side *DF*, and side *BC* is dilated to get side *EF*. Side *AB* **corresponds** to side *DE*, that is, they are **corresponding sides**. Notice that vertex *A* corresponds to vertex *D*, *C* to *F*, and *B* to *E*.

Not all correspondences are so easily seen. Sometimes you have to rotate or reflect the shapes mentally so that you can tell which parts are the corresponding sides, angles, or vertices. For example, the two triangles at right are similar, with *R* corresponding to *X*, *S* to *Y*, and *T* to *Z*. You can get triangle *XYZ* from triangle *RST* by a dilation of $\frac{1}{2}$ followed by a 90° counter-clockwise (↺) turn.

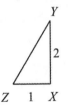

Shapes that are similar and have the same size are called **congruent**. Congruent shapes have corresponding sides of equal length and corresponding angles of equal measure. Rigid transformations (reflections, rotations, and translations), along with dilations with a multiplier of 1 or -1, create congruent shapes.

SCALE FACTOR

A **scale factor** is a ratio that describes how two quantities or lengths are related. A scale factor that describes how two similar shapes are related can be found by writing a ratio between any pair of corresponding sides as $\frac{new}{original}$.

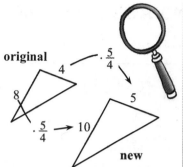

For example, the two similar triangles at right are related by a scale factor of $\frac{5}{4}$ because the side lengths of the new triangle can be found by multiplying the corresponding side lengths of the original triangle by $\frac{5}{4}$.

A scale factor greater than one **enlarges** a shape (makes it larger). A scale factor between zero and one **reduces** a shape (makes it smaller). If a scale factor is equal to one, the two similar shapes are identical and are called **congruent**.

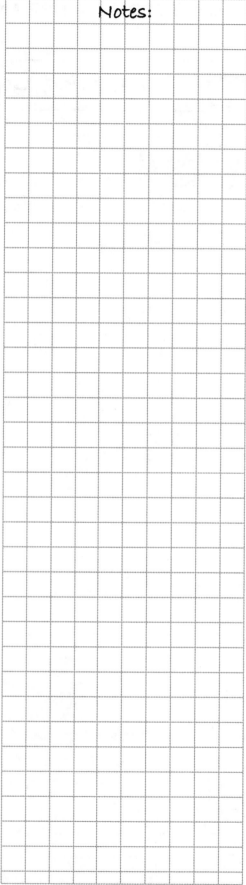

Notes:

Date:	Learning Log Title:
Lesson:	

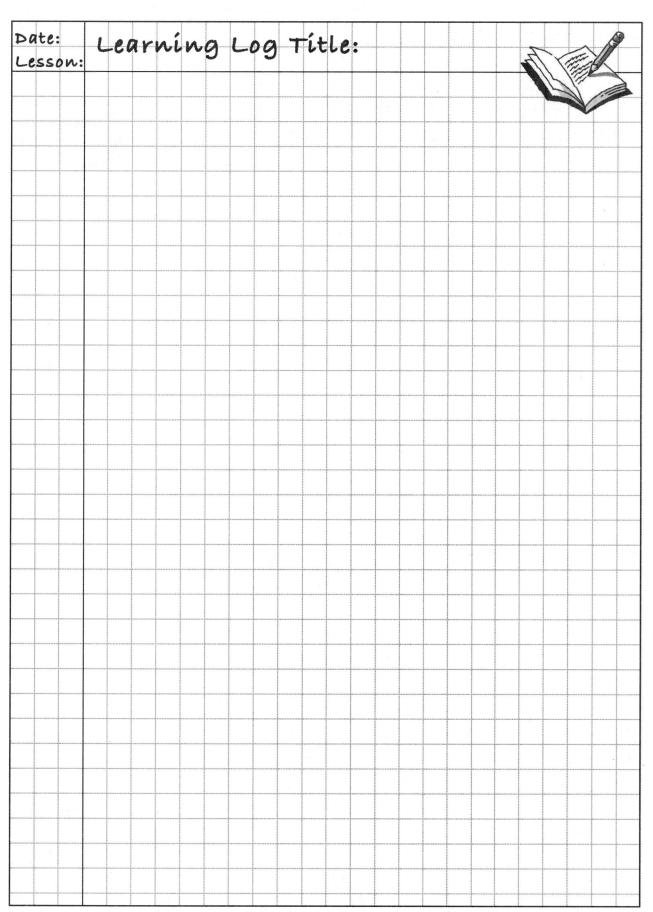

Date: Lesson:	Learning Log Title:

Date: Lesson:	Learning Log Title: 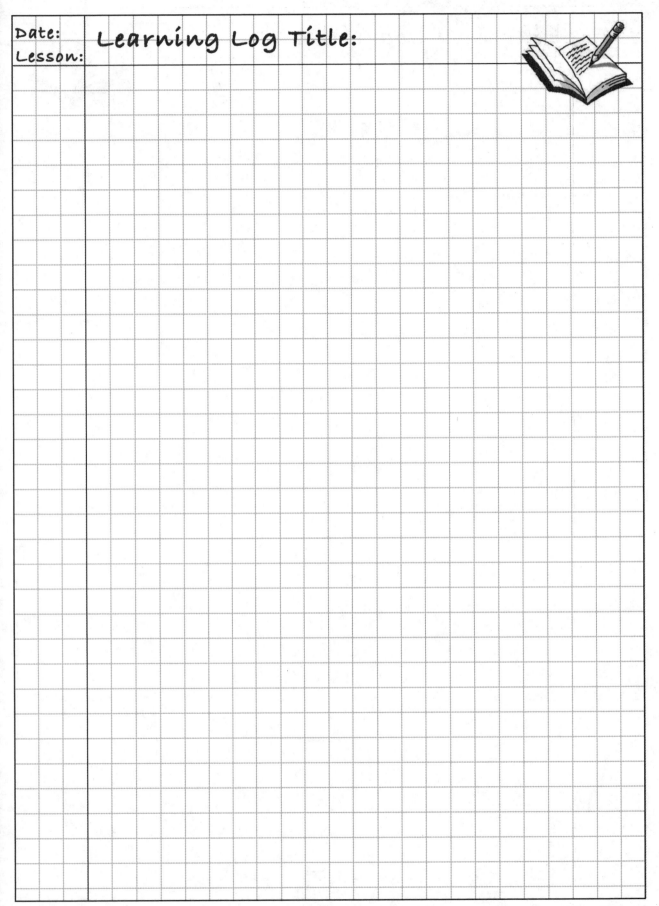

Date: Lesson:	Learning Log Title:

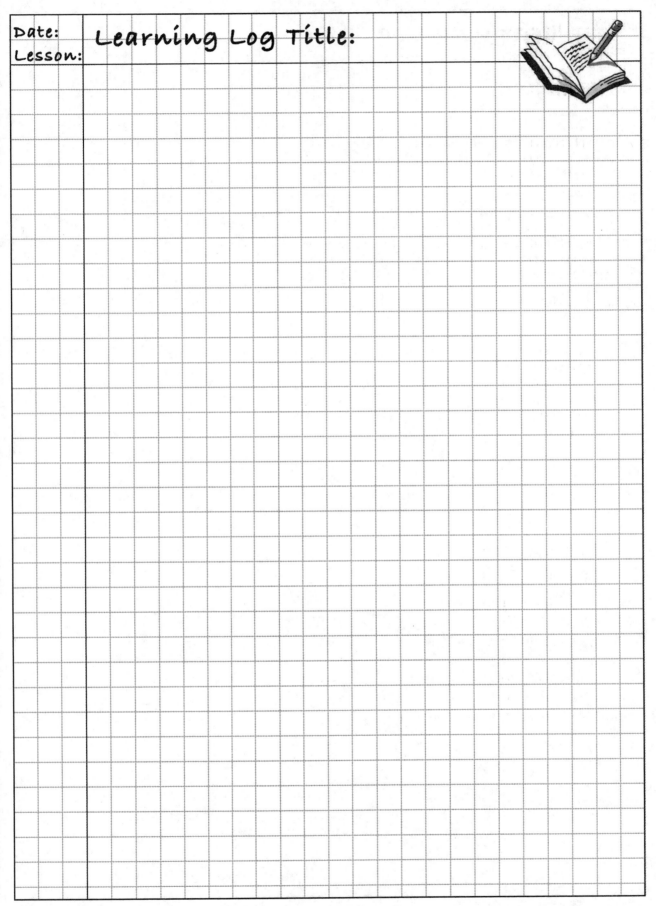

Date:

Lesson:

Learning Log Title:

MATH NOTES

CIRCLE GRAPHS

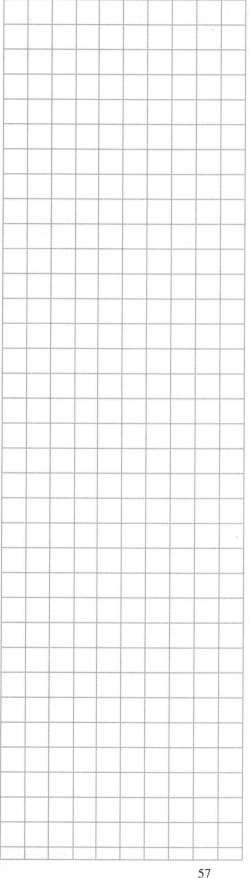

A **circle graph** (sometimes called a **pie chart**) is similar to a bar graph in that it deals with categorical data (such as make of car or grade in school) and not continuous data (such as age or height).

Each category of data is put into its own sector of the circle. The measure of the central angle bounding the sector is proportional to the percent of elements of that type of the whole. For example, if Central Schools has 40% of its students in elementary school, 35% in middle school, and 25% in high

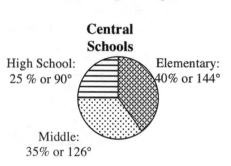

Central Schools

High School:
25 % or 90°

Elementary:
40% or 144°

Middle:
35% or 126°

school, then its circle graph would have a central angle of 144° (0.4 times 360°) for the sector showing the elementary school, 126° for the sector showing the elementary school, and 90° for the sector showing the high school.

LINE OF BEST FIT

A **line of best fit** is a straight line drawn through the center of a group of data points plotted on a scatterplot. It represents a set of data for two variables. It does not need to intersect each data point. Rather, it needs to approximate the data. A line of best fit looks and "behaves" like the data, as shown in the example at right.

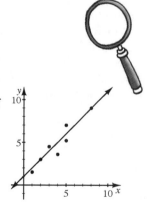

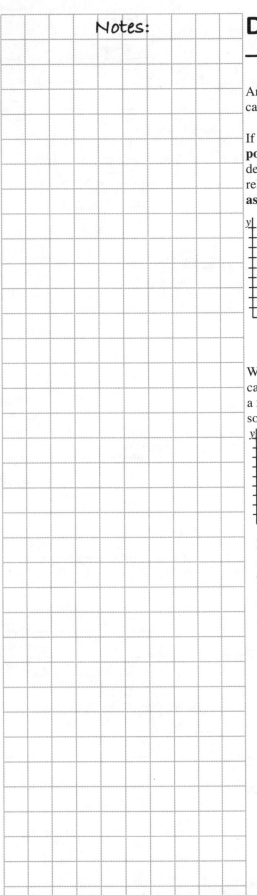

Notes:

DESCRIBING ASSOCIATION – PART 1

An association (relationship) between two numerical variables can be described by its form, direction, strength, and outliers.

If one variable increases as the other variable increases, there is said to be a **positive association**. If one variable increases as the other variable decreases, there is said to be a **negative association**. If there is no relationship between the variables, then the points in the scatterplot have **no association**. An example of each situation is illustrated below.

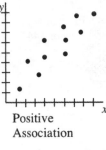

Positive
Association

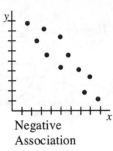

Negative
Association

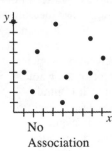

No
Association

When there is a positive or negative association, the shape of the pattern is called the **form** of the association. Associations can have a **linear form** or a **non-linear-form**, and the form can be made up of **clusters** of data. See some examples below.

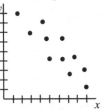

Negative **linear** association (for example, gas mileage decreases as the weight of cargo on a truck increases)

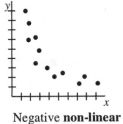

Negative **non-linear** association (for example, temperature of a cup of coffee decreases over time)

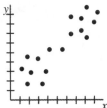

Positive **linear** association with **clusters** (for example, height increases as shoe size increases; one cluster is mostly girls and the other cluster is mostly boys)

SLOPE OF A LINE

The **slope** of a line is the ratio of the change in y to the change in x between any two points on the line. To find slope, you compute the *ratio* that indicates how y-values are changing with respect to x-values. Essentially, slope is the unit rate of change, because it measures how much y increases or decreases as x changes by one unit. If the slope is positive (+), the y-values are increasing. If it is negative (–), the y-values are decreasing. The graph of a line goes up for positive slopes and down for negatives slopes as the line moves across the graph from left to right.

$$\text{slope} = \frac{\text{vertical change}}{\text{horizontal change}} = \frac{\text{change in } y\text{-values}}{\text{change in } x\text{-values}}$$

Some textbooks write this ratio as $\frac{\text{rise}}{\text{run}}$.

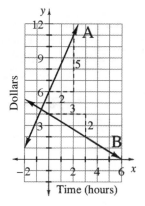

In the graph at right, the slope of line A is $\frac{5 \text{ dollars}}{2 \text{ hours}}$ because for every 2 hours the line increases horizontally, the line increases 5 dollars vertically. Since y increases by $\frac{5}{2}$ dollars when x increases by 1 hour, the unit rate is $\frac{\frac{5}{2} \text{ dollars}}{1 \text{ hour}}$ or 2.5 dollars per hour.

To find the slope of line B, notice that when x increases by 3 hours, y *decreases* by 2 dollars, so the vertical change is –2 dollars and the slope is written as $-\frac{2 \text{ dollars}}{3 \text{ hours}}$ or $-\frac{2}{3}$ dollars per hour.

It is important to notice that horizontal lines do not increase or decrease vertically, so they are described with a slope of 0. The slope of a vertical line is undefined. This is because the horizontal change is 0, resulting in a slope of $\frac{y}{0}$, which is undefined.

slope = 0   slope is undefined

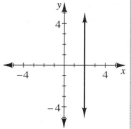

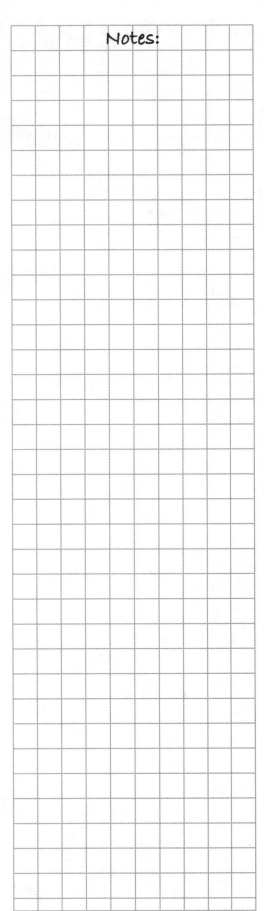

Notes:

PROPORTIONAL EQUATIONS

A proportional relationship can be seen in a table or a graph, as you saw in Section 1.2 of Chapter 1. The equation for a proportion is $y = kx$, where k is the **constant of proportionality**, or the slope of the line. The starting point of the linear equation is always zero, because a proportional relationship always passes through the origin.

The constant of proportionality, when written as a fraction with a denominator of 1, is the **unit rate**.

For example, if the constant of proportionality (the slope) is $\frac{\$7.00}{3 \text{ pounds chicken}}$, then the equation relating weight to cost is $y = \frac{7}{3}x$, where x is the weight (lbs) and y is the cost (\$).

The unit rate is $\frac{\$\frac{7}{3}}{1 \text{ pound chicken}} \approx \$2.33$ per pound.

DESCRIBING ASSOCIATION – PART 2

Although considering the direction of an association (positive or negative) is important in describing it, it is just as important to consider the **strength** of the association. Strength is a description of how much scatter there is in the data away from the line of best fit. Examples are shown below.

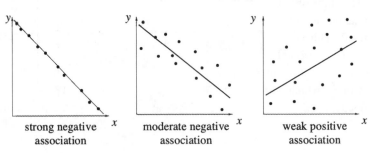

strong negative   moderate negative   weak positive
association   association   association

An **outlier** is a piece of data that does not seem to fit into the pattern. There is one obvious outlier in the association on the graph at right.

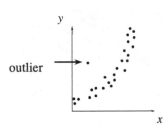

outlier

Core Connections, Course 3

CHAPTER 8: EXPONENTS AND FUNCTIONS

Date: Lesson:	Learning Log Title:

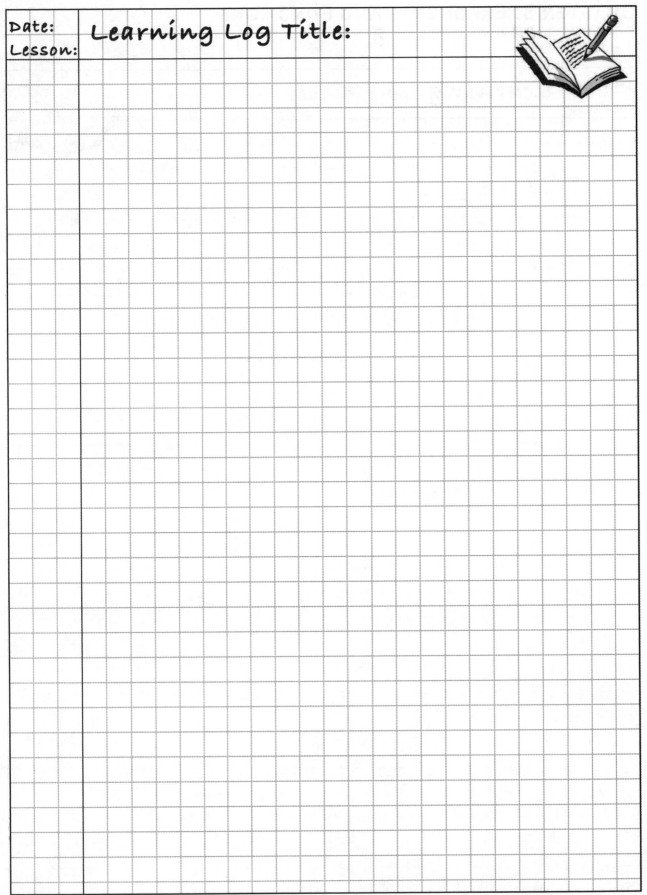

Date: Lesson:	Learning Log Title:

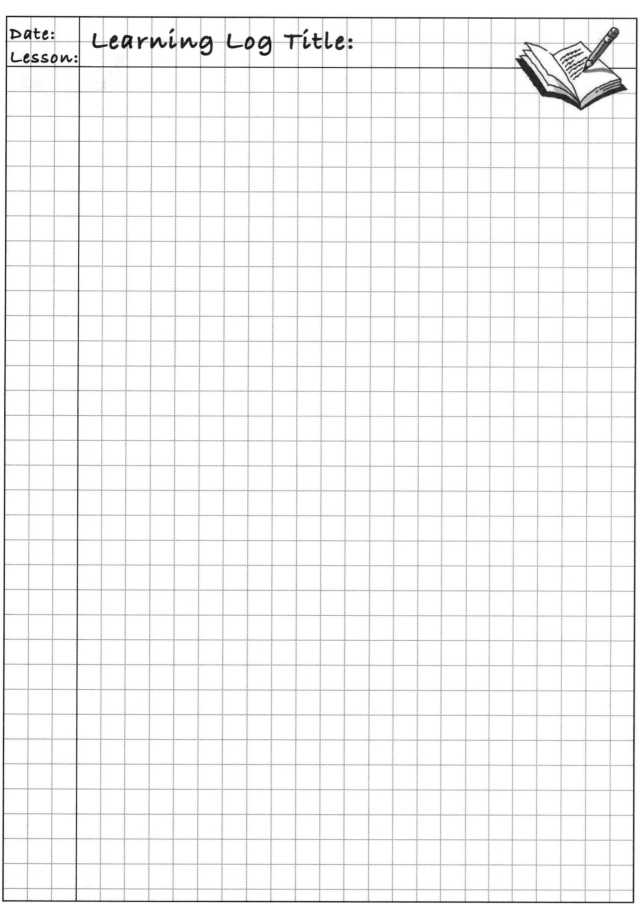

Date: Lesson:	Learning Log Title:

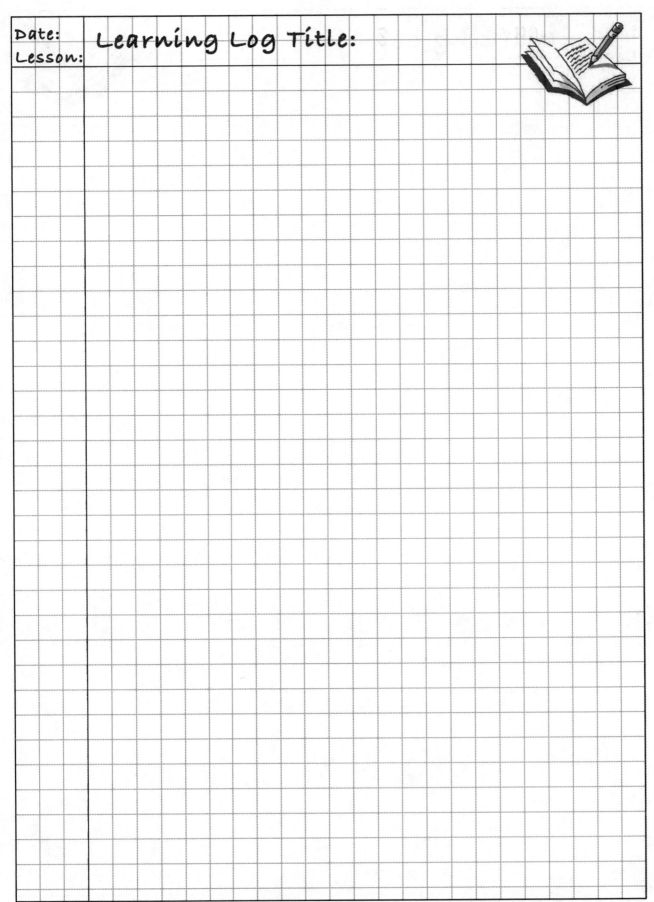

Date:
Lesson:

Learning Log Title:

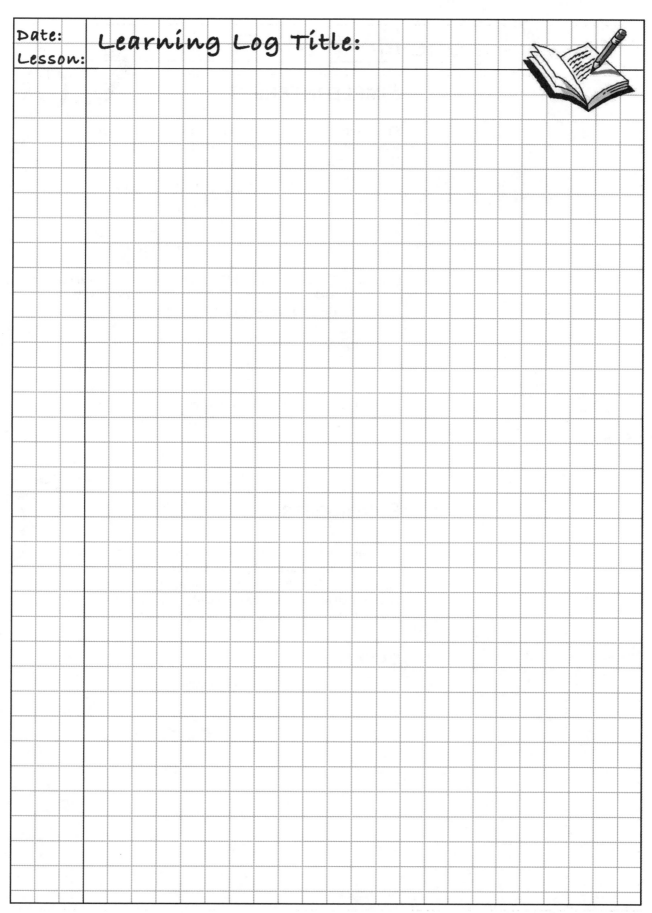

| Date: | Learning Log Title: |
| Lesson: | |

MATH NOTES

SIMPLE INTEREST

Simple interest is interest paid only on the original amount of the principal at each specified interval (such as annually, or monthly). The formula to calculate simple interest is:

$$I = Prt \qquad \text{where} \qquad \begin{aligned} P &= \text{Principal} \\ I &= \text{Interest} \\ r &= \text{Rate} \\ t &= \text{Time} \end{aligned}$$

Example: Theresa invested $1425.00 in a savings account at her local bank. The bank pays a simple interest rate of 3.5% annually. How much money will Theresa have after 4 years?

$$I = Prt \qquad \Rightarrow \quad I = 1425(0.035)(4) = \$199.50$$
$$\qquad \Rightarrow \quad P + I = \$1425 + \$199.50 = \$1624.50$$

Theresa will have $1624.50 after 4 years.

EXPONENTS

Bases and exponents can be used to rewrite expressions that involve repeated multiplication by the same number or variable. The expression a^n is written in **exponent form**. The **base**, a, is a factor that is raised to a power. The **exponent**, n, is sometimes called the power. It shows how many times the base is used as a factor.

In general, a^n means a multiplied by itself n times.

For example, 2^4 means $2 \cdot 2 \cdot 2 \cdot 2$.

The base is 2 and the exponent is 4.

COMPOUND INTEREST

Compound interest is interest paid on both the original principal (amount of money at the start) and the interest earned previously.

The formula for compound interest is: $A = P(1+r)^n$ where

> A = total amount including previous interest earned,
> P = principal,
> r = interest rate for each compounding period, and
> n = number of time periods

Example: Theresa has a student loan that charges a 1.5% monthly compound interest rate. If she currently owes $1425.00 and does not make a payment for a year, how much will she owe at the end of the year (12 months)?

$$A = P(1+r)^n \implies \quad A = 1425(1+0.015)^{12}$$

$$\implies \quad 1425(1.015)^{12} = 1425 \cdot 1.1956 = \$1703.73$$

Theresa will owe $1703.73 after 12 months (1 year).

SCIENTIFIC NOTATION

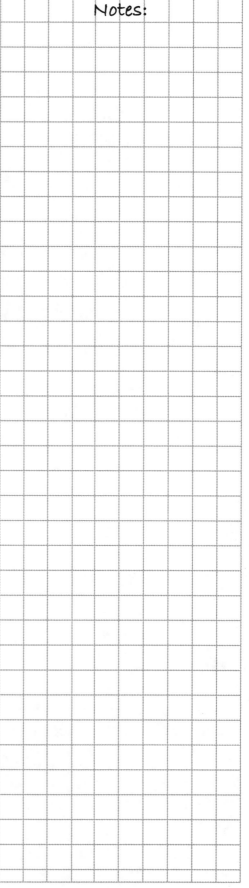

Scientific notation is a way of writing very large and very small numbers compactly. A number is said to be in scientific notation when it is written as a product of two factors as described below.

The first factor is less than 10 and greater than or equal to 1.

The second factor has a base of 10 and an integer exponent.

The factors are separated by a multiplication sign.

Scientific Notation	Standard Form
5.32×10^6	5,320,000
3.07×10^{-4}	0.000307
2.61×10^{-15}	0.00000000000000261

Notes:

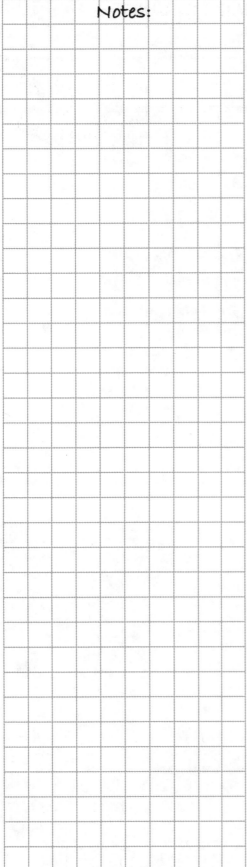

Notes:

LAWS OF EXPONENTS

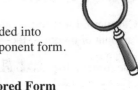

Expressions that include exponents can be expanded into factored form and then rewritten in simplified exponent form.

Expression	**Factored Form**
$(5x)^3(2y)(x^2)y$	$5 \cdot x \cdot 5 \cdot x \cdot 5 \cdot x \cdot 2 \cdot y \cdot x \cdot x \cdot y$

Simplified Exponent Form
$$250x^5y^2$$

The **Laws of Exponents** summarize several rules for simplifying expressions that have exponents. The rules below are true if $x \neq 0$ and $y \neq 0$.

$$x^a \cdot x^b = x^{(a+b)} \qquad (x^a)^b = x^{ab} \qquad \frac{x^a}{x^b} = x^{(a-b)}$$

$$x^0 = 1 \qquad (x^a y^b)^c = x^{ac}y^{bc} \qquad x^{-a} = \frac{1}{x^a}$$

FUNCTIONS

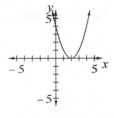

A relationship between inputs and outputs is a **function** if there is no more than one output for each input. A function is often written in a form where y is set equal to some expression involving x. In this "$y =$" form, x is the input and y is the output. Below is an example of a function.

$$y = (x-2)^2$$

x	-2	-1	0	1	2	3	4	5
y	16	9	4	1	0	1	4	9

In the example above the value of y depends on x. Therefore, y is called the **dependent variable** and x is called the **independent variable**.

The equation $x^2 + y^2 = 1$ is not a function because there are two y-values (outputs) for some x-values, as shown below.

$$x^2 + y^2 = 1$$

x	-1	0	0	1
y	0	-1	1	0

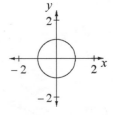

CHAPTER 9: ANGLES AND PYTHAGOREAN THEOREM

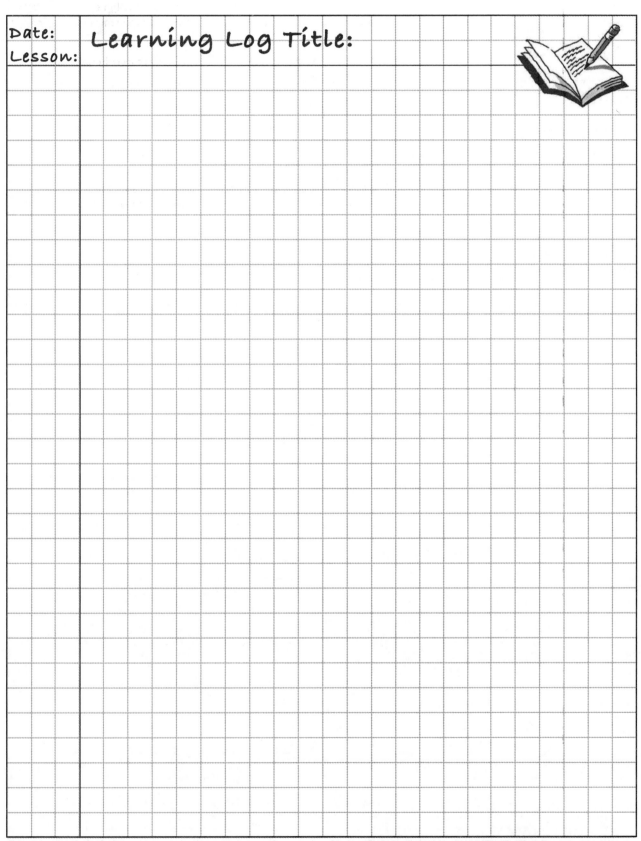

Date: Lesson:	Learning Log Title:

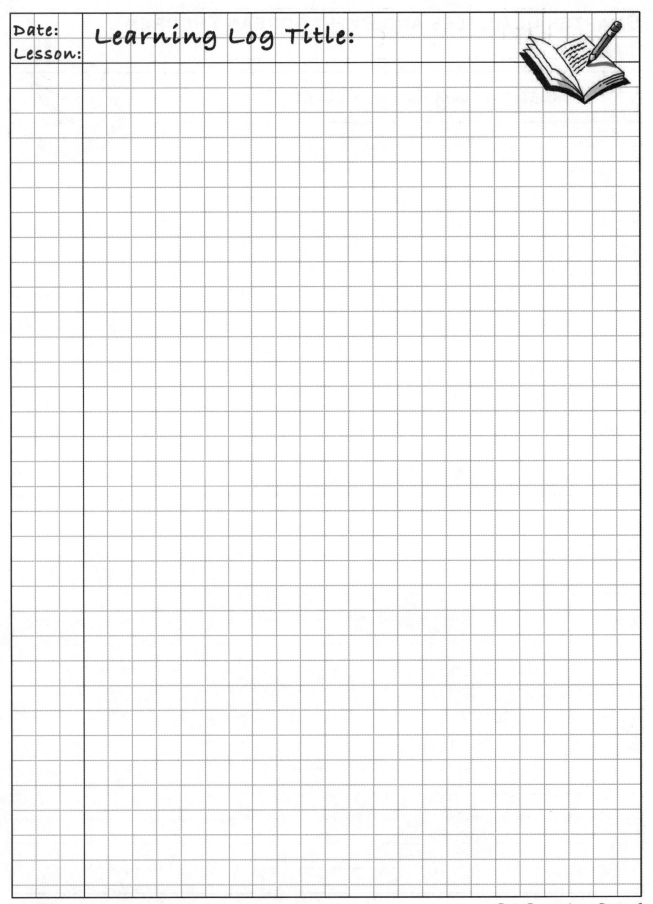

Date:

Lesson:

Learning Log Title:

Date: Lesson:	Learning Log Title:

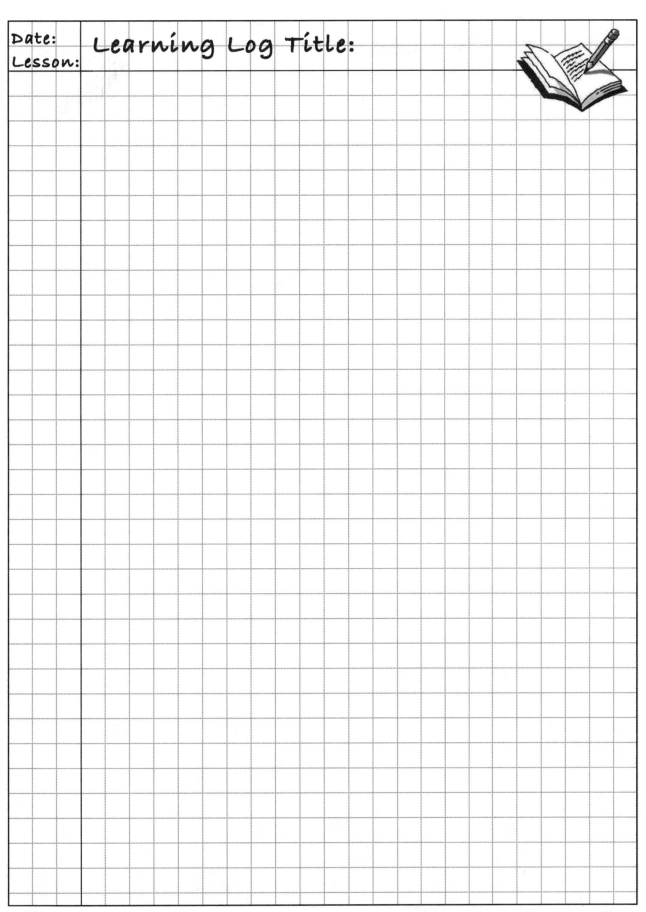

Date:	Learning Log Title:
Lesson:	

Date: Lesson:	Learning Log Title:

Date:	Learning Log Title:
Lesson:	

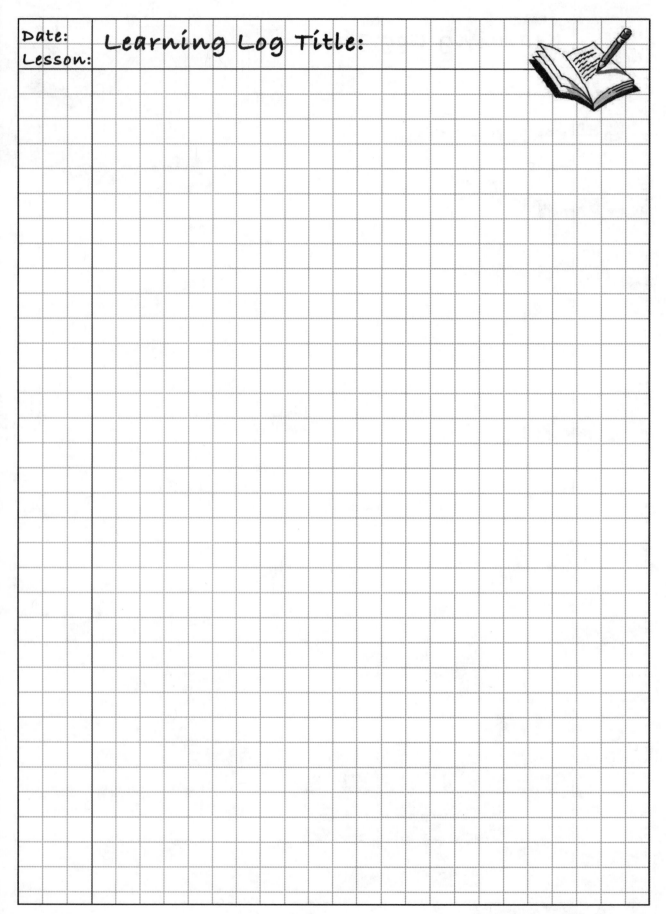

Date: Lesson:	Learning Log Title:

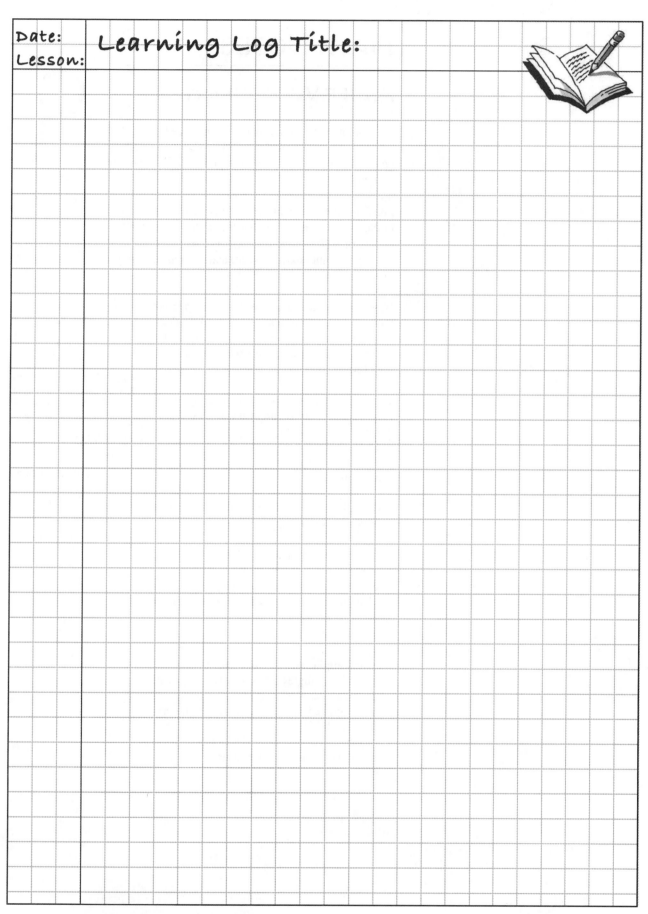

Notes:

MATH NOTES

ANGLE VOCABULARY

It is common to identify angles using three letters. For example, $\angle ABC$ means the angle you would find by going from point A to point B to point C in the diagram at right.

Point B is the **vertex** of the angle (where the endpoints of the two sides meet), and BA and BC are the rays that define it. A **ray** is a part of a line that has an endpoint (starting point) and extends infinitely in one direction.

If two angles have measures that add up to 90°, they are called **complementary angles**. For example, in the diagram above, $\angle ABC$ and $\angle CBD$ are complementary because together they form a right angle.

Complementary

If two angles have measures that add up to 180°, they are called **supplementary angles**. For example, in the diagram at right, $\angle EFG$ and $\angle GFH$ are supplementary because together they form a **straight angle** (that is, together they form a line).

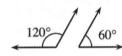

Supplementary

Two angles do not have to share a vertex to be complementary or supplementary.

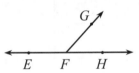

Adjacent angles are angles that have a common vertex, share a common side, and have no interior points in common. So angles $\angle c$ and $\angle d$ in the diagram at right are adjacent angles, as are $\angle c$ and $\angle f$, $\angle f$ and $\angle g$, and $\angle g$ and $\angle d$.

Vertical angles are the two opposite (that is, non-adjacent) angles formed by two intersecting lines, such as angles $\angle c$ and $\angle g$ in the diagram above right. By itself, $\angle c$ is not a vertical angle, nor is $\angle g$, although $\angle c$ and $\angle g$ together are a pair of vertical angles. Vertical angles always have equal measure.

PARALLEL LINES AND ANGLE PAIRS

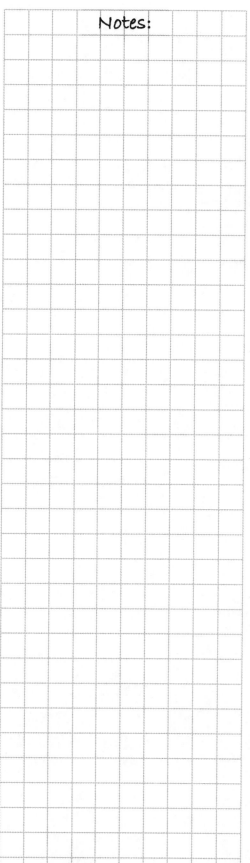

Corresponding angles lie in the same position but at different points of intersection of the transversal. For example, in the diagram at right, $\angle m$ and $\angle d$ form a pair of corresponding angles, since both of them are to the right of the transversal and above the intersecting line. Corresponding angles are congruent when the lines intersected by the transversal are parallel.

$\angle f$ and $\angle m$ are **alternate interior angles** because one is to the left of the transversal, one is to the right, and both are between (inside) the pair of lines. Alternate interior angles are congruent when the lines intersected by the transversal are parallel.

$\angle g$ and $\angle m$ are **same side interior angles** because both are on the same side of the transversal and both are between the pair of lines. Same side interior angles are supplementary when the lines intersected by the transversal are parallel.

ANGLE SUM THEOREM FOR TRIANGLES

The measures of the angles in a triangle add up to 180°. For example, in $\triangle ABC$ at right, $m\angle A + m\angle B + m\angle C = 180°$.

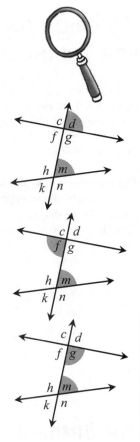

You can verify this statement by carefully drawing a triangle with a ruler, tearing off two of the angles ($\angle A$ and $\angle B$), and placing them side by side with the third angle ($\angle C$) on a straight line. The sum of the three angles is the same as the straight angle (line), that is, 180°.

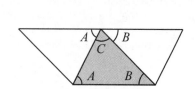

EXTERIOR ANGLE THEOREM FOR TRIANGLES

An **exterior angle** of a triangle is an angle outside of the triangle created by extending one of the sides of the triangle. In the diagram at right, $\angle 4$ is an exterior angle.

The **Exterior Angle Theorem for Triangles** states that the measure of the exterior angle of a triangle is equal to the sum of the **remote interior angles**. In the diagram, $\angle 1$ and $\angle 2$ are the remote interior angles to $\angle 4$. Note that some texts call these angles "opposite interior angles." n symbols:

$$m\angle 4 = m\angle 1 + m\angle 2$$

AA SIMILARITY FOR TRIANGLES

For two triangles to be similar, corresponding angles must have equal measure.

However, it is sufficient to know that two pairs of corresponding angles have equal measures, because then the third pair of angles must have equal measure.

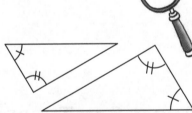

AA ~ : If two pairs of corresponding angles have equal measure, then the triangles are similar.

This is known as the **Angle-Angle Triangle Similarity Conjecture**, which can be abbreviated as "AA Similarity" or "AA ~."

Notes:

TRIANGLE INEQUALITY AND SIDE LENGTH PATTERNS

The **Triangle Inequality** establishes the required relationships for three lengths to form a triangle. You can also use these lengths to determine the type of triangle they form — acute, obtuse, or right — by comparing the squares of the lengths of the sides as described below.

For any three lengths to form a triangle, the sum of the lengths of any two sides must be greater than the length of the third side.

For example, the lengths 3 cm, 10 cm, and 11 cm will form a triangle, because:

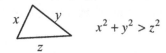

$$3 + 10 > 11$$

$$3 + 11 > 10$$

$$10 + 11 > 3$$

The lengths 5 m, 7 m, and 15 m will not form a triangle, because $5 + 7 = 12$, and $12 \not> 15$.

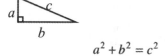

Acute triangle: The sum of the squares of the lengths of the two shorter sides is greater than the square of the length of the longest side.

$$x^2 + y^2 > z^2$$

Obtuse triangle: The sum of the squares of the lengths of the two shorter sides is less than the square of the length of the longest side.

$$p^2 + q^2 < r^2$$

Right triangle: The sum of the squares of the lengths of the two shorter sides is equal to the square of the length of the longest side.

$$a^2 + b^2 = c^2$$

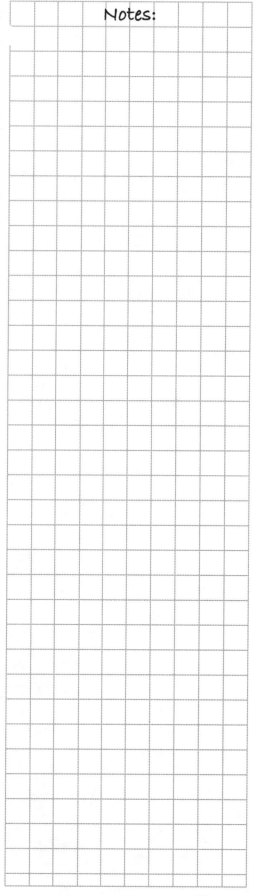

Notes:

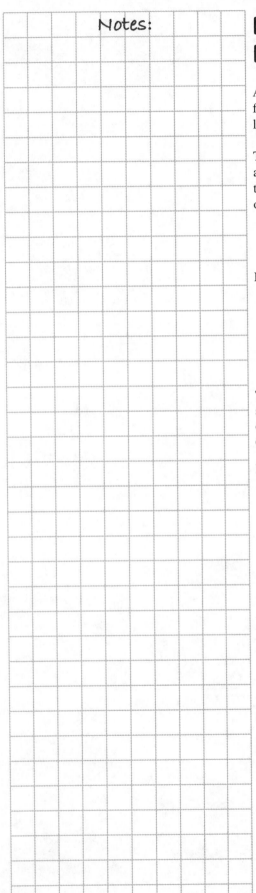

Notes:

RIGHT TRIANGLES AND THE PYTHAGOREAN THEOREM

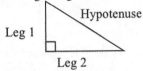

A right triangle is a triangle in which the two shorter sides form a right (90°) angle. The shorter sides are called **legs**. The third and longest side, called the **hypotenuse**, is opposite the right angle.

The **Pythagorean Theorem** states that for any right triangle, the sum of the squares of the lengths of the legs is equal to the square of the length of the hypotenuse.

$$(\text{leg } 1)^2 + (\text{leg } 2)^2 = (\text{hypotenuse})^2$$

Example:

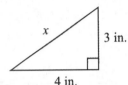

The **converse of the Pythagorean Theorem** states that if the sum of the squares of the lengths of the two shorter sides of a triangle equals the square of the length of the longest side, then the triangle is a right triangle. For example:

Do the lengths 6, 9, and 11 form a right triangle?

$$6^2 + 9^2 \overset{?}{=} 11^2$$

$$36 + 81 \overset{?}{=} 121$$

$$117 \neq 121$$

No, these lengths do not form a right triangle.

Do the lengths 9, 40, and 41 form a right triangle?

$$9^2 + 40^2 \overset{?}{=} 41^2$$

$$81 + 1600 \overset{?}{=} 1681$$

$$1681 = 1681$$

Yes, these lengths form a right triangle.

THE REAL-NUMBER SYSTEM

The **real numbers** include all of the **rational numbers** and **irrational numbers**.

Rational numbers are numbers that can be written as a fraction in the form $\frac{p}{q}$, where p and q are integers and $q \neq 0$. Rational numbers written in decimal form either terminate or repeat. The number 7 is a rational number, because it can be written as $\frac{7}{1}$. The number –0.687 is rational, because it can be written as $-\frac{687}{1000}$. Even $\sqrt{25}$ is rational, because it can be written as $\frac{5}{1}$. Other examples of rational numbers include –12, 0, 3, $\frac{1}{8}$, $\frac{5}{9}$, 0.25, and $\sqrt{81}$.

Irrational numbers are numbers that cannot be written as fractions. Decimals that do not terminate or repeat are irrational numbers. For example, $\sqrt{3}$ is an irrational number. It cannot be written as a fraction, and when it is written as a decimal, it neither terminates nor repeats ($\sqrt{3} \approx 1.73205080756...$). Other irrational numbers include $\sqrt{2}$, $\sqrt{7}$, and π.

SQUARING AND SQUARE ROOTS

When a number or variable is multiplied by itself, it is said to be **squared**. Squaring a number is like finding the area of the square with that number or variable as its side length. For example:

$6 \cdot 6 = 6^2 = 36$
and

| 36 cm^2 | 6 cm |

6 cm

$a \cdot a = a^2$
and

| a^2 | a |

a

The **square root** of a number or variable is the positive factor that, when multiplied by itself, results in the given number. Use a **radical sign**, $\sqrt{\ }$, to show this operation. If you know the area of a square, then the square root of the numerical value of the area is the side length of that square.

For example, $\sqrt{49}$ is read as, "the square root of 49," and means, "Find the positive number that multiplied by itself equals 49." $\sqrt{49} = 7$, since $7 \cdot 7 = 49$.

By definition, –7 is not the square root of 49 even though $(-7) \cdot (-7) = 49$, since only consider positive numbers are considered to be square roots. No real square region could have a negative side length.

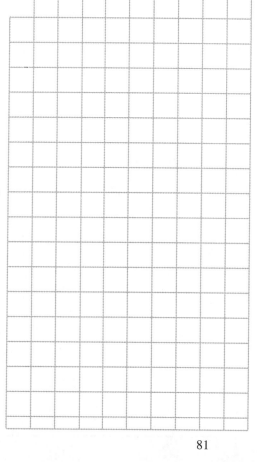

Notes:

CHAPTER 10: SURFACE AREA AND VOLUME

Date: Lesson:	Learning Log Title:

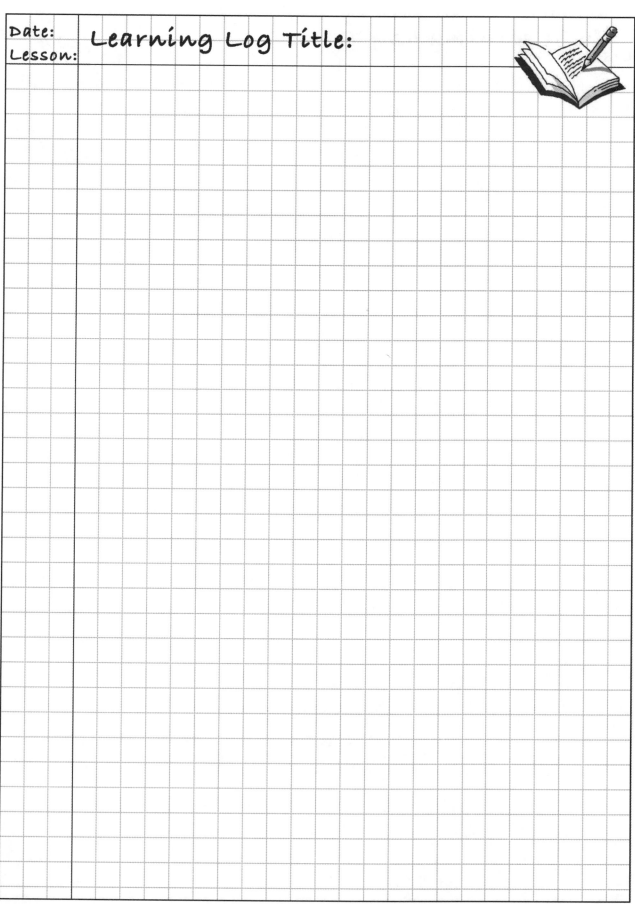

Date:	Learning Log Title:
Lesson:	

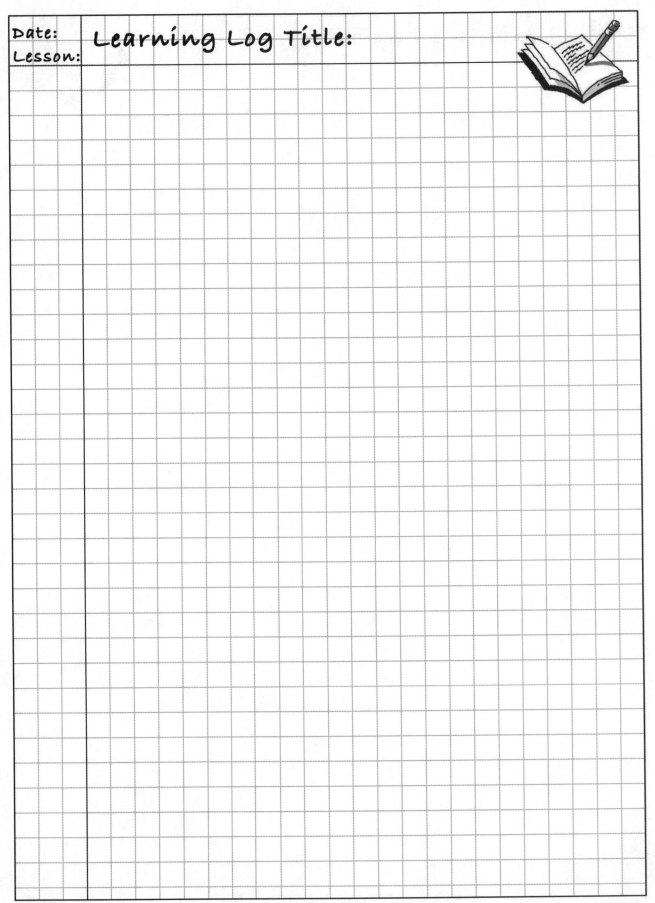

Date:

Lesson:

Learning Log Title:

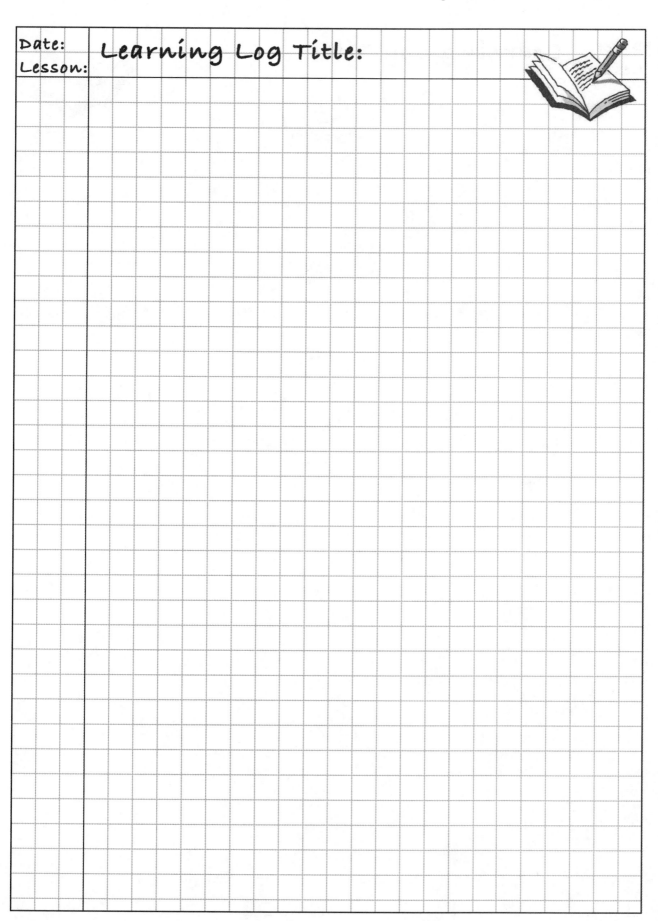

Date: Lesson:	Learning Log Title:

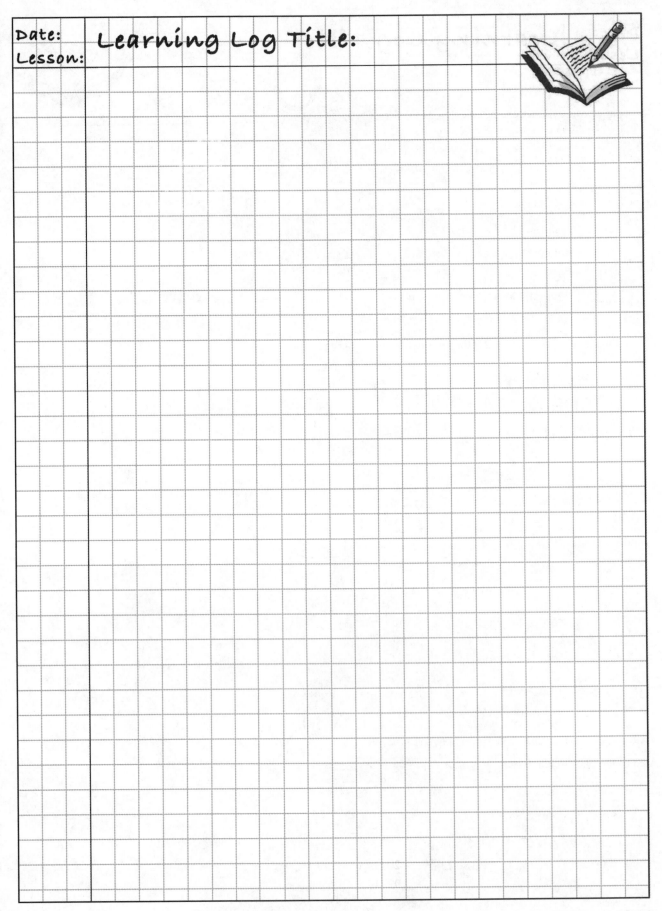

Date:	Learning Log Title:
Lesson:	

MATH NOTES

VOLUME OF A CYLINDER

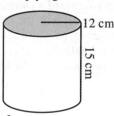

The volume of a cylinder can be calculated in exactly the same way as the volume of a prism. First divide the cylinder into layers that are each one unit high. Then, to calculate the total volume, multiply the volume of one layer by the number of layers it takes to fill the shape.

The volume of a cylinder can also be calculated by multiplying the area of the base (B) by the height (h).

$$\text{Volume} = (\text{area of base})(\text{height})$$

$$V = Bh = (r^2\pi)(h)$$

For example, for the cylinder at right:

Area of the base: $B = (12)^2\pi = 144\pi$ cm^2

Volume: $V = 144\pi(15) = 2160\pi \approx 6785.84$ cm^3

SURFACE AREA OF A CYLINDER

A **cylinder** has two congruent, circular bases. The **lateral surface** of the cylinder, when opened flat, forms a rectangle with a height equal to the height of the cylinder and a width equal to the circumference of the cylinder's base.

The surface area of a cylinder is the sum of the two base areas and the lateral surface area. The formula for the surface area is:

circumference

$$S.A. = 2r^2\pi + \pi dh$$

$$= 2r^2\pi + 2\pi rh$$

where r = radius, d = diameter, and h = height of the cylinder.

lateral
face
(rectangle)

For example, to find the surface area of the cylinder below:

Area of the two circular bases:

$2(28 \text{ cm})^2\pi = 1568\pi$ cm^2

Area of the lateral face:

$\pi(56)(25) = 1400\pi$ cm^2

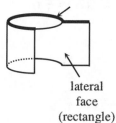

Total surface area = 1568π cm$^2 + 1400\pi$ cm$^2 = 2968\pi$ cm^2

≈ 9324.25 cm^2

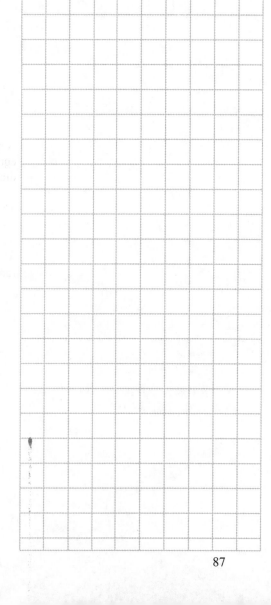

VOLUME OF A PYRAMID AND A CONE

In general, the **volume of a pyramid** is one-third of the volume of the prism with the same base area and height. Thus:

$$V = \tfrac{1}{3}(\text{base area})(\text{height})$$

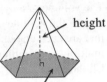

The **volume of a cone** is one-third of the volume of the cylinder with the same radius and height. Therefore, the volume of a cone can be found using the formula shown below, where r is the radius of the base and h is the height of the cone.

$$V = \tfrac{1}{3}(\text{base area})(\text{height}) = \tfrac{1}{3}\pi r^2 h$$

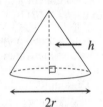

VOLUME OF A SPHERE

A **sphere** is formed by a set of points that are equidistant from a fixed point, its center. It is three-dimensional.

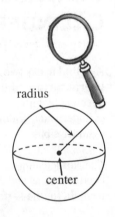

The volume of a sphere is twice the volume of a cone with the same radius and height. Since the volume of a cone with radius r and height $2r$ is $V = \tfrac{1}{3}\pi r^2(2r) = \tfrac{2}{3}\pi r^3$, the volume of a sphere with radius r is:

$$V = \tfrac{4}{3}\pi r^3$$